NPA PERSONALITY THEORY
IN IMAGES

NPA PERSONALITY THEORY
IN IMAGES

A.M. BENIS, Sc.D., M.D.

A.M. BENIS
New York

A wise man once observed that if you study an object of nature intently enough, if you focus upon it long enough all your powers of concentration and attention, there comes a point at which the macrocosm behind the object is suddenly revealed — in somewhat the way in which the vista beyond a keyhole is magnified if one purposefully advances one's eye toward it.

— Bernard Rimland (1964)

CONTENTS

ILLUSTRATIONS   ix

PREFACE   xv

PART ONE: Theory   1

PART TWO: Sanguinity: The N Trait   13

PART THREE: Perfectionism: The P Trait   29

PART FOUR: Aggression: The A Trait   39

PART FIVE: Inhibition of Aggression:
        Passive Aggressive Types   53

PART SIX: Inversions:
        Pseudo-Aggression and Pseudo-Narcissism   59

PART SEVEN: Caricatures of the Character Types   63

PART EIGHT: Historical Figures   101

PART NINE: Couples   113

PART TEN: Children of the World   125

PART ELEVEN: Origins and Geography   141

PART TWELVE: Diversity and Disability   173

APPENDIX: Synopsis of NPA Theory   192

Glossary   210

Sources of Illustrations   216

Bibliography   227

About the author   227

ILLUSTRATIONS

PART 1 — Theory

1   Venn diagram of NPA types.

2   The N and A rages.

3   The ancient theory of humors.

4   Robert Fludd's "Mind of the Microcosm".

5   The Punnett Square.

6   "The die is cast": the basis of personality is genetic.

7   Progeny chart.

8   The enigma of short parents with tall children.

9   Tall bridal couple with short parents.

10   Tall NP type and short A type.

11   The NPA personality test.

PART 2 — Sanguinity: The N Trait

12   Gingival smile of sanguinity.

13   Response to recognition on the stage.

14   Greeting a friend.

15   Gestures: the Narcissistic Arms Pose.

16   Gestures: a child shows a pose of recognition.

17   Gestures: the Joan of Arc Pose.

18   Gestures: Hallelujah!

19   Gestures: a smile by another name.

20   The sanguine "selfie".

21   Blushing.

22   Tearfulness.

23   Tattoo exhibitionism.

24   "Showing off" exhibitionism.

25   Narcissus!

26   Showtime!

PART 3 — Perfectionism: The P Trait

27   Florence Cathedral.

28   Korean gymnastics festival.

29   Terracotta Army.

30   Beetle collection.

31   Music: presence and absence of P trait.

32   Surgical masks in public.

33   K-pop: the N and P traits together.

34   Black rectangular eyeglasses.

35   Colorful apparel: absence of P trait.

PART 4 — Aggression: The A Trait

36   Non-sanguine aggression.

37   Non-sanguine grins and laughs.

38   Gestures: the intimidating glare.

39   Gestures: the aggressive finger point.

40   Eye contact of dominance and submission.

41   Gestures: the clenched fist.

42   Confrontational pose of aggression.

43   Gestures: the choke.

44   Violence!

45   Non-sanguine meets sanguine: the non-sanguine "selfie".

46   Sanguine meets non-sanguine: espousal in Latvia.

47   N and A traits come together: the NA type.

48   N, P and A traits all come together: the NPA type.

PART 5 — Inhibition of Aggression: Passive Aggressive Types

49   Shyness in a child.

50   Camera-shy.

51   Camera aversion.

52   Mugging for the camera.

53   Stage fright.

PART 6 — Inversions: Pseudo-Aggression and -Narcissism

54   Pseudo-aggression: the Goth girl.

55   Pseudo-narcissism: adornment in a non-sanguine type.

56   Pseudo-narcissism: Boy George, then and now.

PART 7 — Caricatures of the Character Types

57   N type: Barack Obama.

58   N type: "Princess".

59   NA type: *Prima donna*.

60   N type: Space cadet.

61   N type: Lady in red.

62   NA type: Lady with pink hair.

63   NA type: Scandalmonger.

64   A type: Vladimir Putin.

65   A type: "Short man syndrome".

66   NP type: Angela Merkel.

67   NP type: "Tall man syndrome".

68   PA type: Power behind the throne, Richard Cheney.

69   PA type: Eastern European female.

70   PA type: False smiler, Nancy Reagan.

71   PA type: the Robert Mitchum look.

72   NPA type: Christopher Christie.

73   NPA type: Virago, Queen of Hearts.

74   NPA type: Matron.

75   NPA type: Warmonger, John Bolton.

76   Pseudo non-sanguinity: Forlorn N type, Chief Phizi Gall.

77   Pseudo non-sanguinity: Antagonized NPA type.

78   NA type: Comic Jerry Lewis.

79   PA type: Sardonic wit Bill Maher.

80   NP type: Cerebral Vulcan, Leonard Nimoy.

81   N type: Showgirl, Josephine Baker.

82   N type: Possessive paramour.

83   N and NA types: Con artist.

84   NA type: the Playboy.

85   NA type: Girthy sexpot.

86   NP type: Middle-aged puritan.

87   NPA− type: Elizabeth Warren.

88   NPA− type: Narendra Modi.

89   NA− type: Michael Jackson.

90   NPA= type: Charles Darwin.

91   NA= type: Battered woman.

92   Resigned type NP−A: the Recluse.

93   Resigned types: Solitude.

PART 8 — Historical Figures

94   Napoleon Bonaparte: N type.

95   Abraham Lincoln: NP type.

96   Mary Lincoln: NA type.

97   Henry VIII: N type.

98   Katherine of Aragon: NP type.

99   Charles I and Cardinal Richelieu: perfectionist types.

100   Friedrich Wilhelm I: NPA type.

101   Rasputin: NA type.

102   Joseph Stalin: A type.

103   Adolf Hitler: NPA− type.

104   Jesus Christ.

PART 9 — Couples

105   NP×NP type: "American Gothic".

106   N×PA type: sanguine and non-sanguine type.

107   Weddings: NPA×NPA and NP×NP type.

108   N×N type: a same-sex relationship.

109   A×N type: pure A and N traits come together.

110   NA×NA type: a non-perfectionistic relationship.

111   Comedy duos: N×NPA and NPA×NPA type.

112   NA×NPA− type: dominance and submission.

113   A×NPA− type: the King of Siam and Anna.

114   Identical twins: identical NPA type.

115   NP type contemplates an alter ego.

PART 10 — Children of the World

116   Sanguine family of N types: Dominican Republic.

117   Sanguine girl, holiday portrait: USA.

118   Non-sanguine girl, holiday portrait: Russia.

119   Madonna and sanguine child: France.

120   Madonna and non-sanguine child: Russia.

121   Non-sanguine boy, a calling to arms: Poland.

122   Sanguine mother with non-sanguine child: USA.

123   Sanguine young ballerina: USA.

124   NP boy with bossy sister: Chile.

125   Elaborate adornment: Ethiopia.

126   Nomadic child of the desert: Sudan.

127   NA boys with aggressive swagger: Zambia.

128   NP polite student with chums: North Korea.

129   NA mother and baby, motif in yellow: USA.

130   Like father, like son: USA.

PART 11 — Origins and Geography

131   Evolutionary origins: other primates.

132   Trait A: aggressive display in a baboon.

133   Trait N: chest-thumping in a gorilla.

134   Trait P: use of tool in chimpanzee.

135   Trait P: grooming in baboons.

136   Trait N: "selfie" smile in an Old World monkey.

137   Trait N: chimpanzee smile.

138   Origins: San Bushmen of southern Africa.

139   Origins: Australian Aborigines.

140   East Africa: Maasai tribesman.

141   West Africa: people of Nigeria.

142   Mongolia: "eagle girl".

143   Eastern Europe: Please do not smile for the camera.

144   Nomadic groups: Bedouin people.

145   Iran: a polymorphic region.

146   Indigenous America: people of the Peruvian Andes.

147   Indigenous America: Dakota People.

148   Polynesia: N types.

149   Maritime Southeast Asia: N types.

150   Mainland southern Asia: N type in Thailand.

151   Melanesia: NA types.

152   Modern America: NA type of African heritage.

153   Modern America: NP farmer of the Midwest.

154   A non-sanguine population: "Authoritarian habitancy".

155   NPA types in a population: successive generations.

156   World map: distribution of P trait.

157   Indian subcontinent and Aboriginal Australia.

158   World map: distribution of non-sanguinity.

159   "Out of Africa" and origin of non-sanguinity.

160   Territoriality and warfare: Aztec example.

161   Slave trade from West Africa: a region of high NA prevalence.

PART 12 — Diversity and Disability

162   Diversity: intimate relationships.

163   Obsessive-compulsive personality.

164   The autistic savant.

165   Antisocial disorder.

166   Sadistic personality.

167   Narcissistic personality.

168   Bipolar disorder.

169   Down's syndrome.

170   Panic disorder.

171   Introversion.

172   Explosive rages.

173   Attention deficit hyperactivity disorder.

174   Post traumatic stress disorder.

175   Parkinson's disease and the A− trait.

176   Eczema and the A− trait.

177   Bulimia and the lack of P trait.

178   Borderline NPA types.

179   Schizophrenia.

PREFACE

If you are already familiar with the NPA model, then the images in this book will be recognized as familiar friends. They will simply be reinforcements to an outlook on life that the model has revealed, one that emphasizes that the human personality is structured on a few identifiable genetic traits. Our hope is that the reader will find the images to be stimulating vignettes, illustrating how the NPA traits can reveal themselves in the most ordinary of circumstances and in so many varied ways.

However, if you are not familiar with the model, then the sequence of the images may seem puzzling. Some of them may appear to be mundane photos of no conceivable importance in a serious treatment of human behavior. In that case, the series of images in this book can serve as a brief introduction to the NPA model itself. With this in mind, we have arranged the images in a coherent sequence, and we have also included a synopsis of the model in the Appendix.

Sometimes there is more to a picture than what first meets the eye. Indeed, if one is willing to focus all the powers of one's concentration, there can come a point at which an image can suddenly be revealed in a different light and to have a deeper meaning. When such a "revelation" occurs, one necessarily passes a threshold of perception where there is no possibility of turning back — one will never again be able to perceive the image in its former, conventional context.

It is a privilege for us to acknowledge the individuals and institutions that permitted reproduction of their works, especially the photographers cited who freely allowed use of their images without obligation. They have our gratitude.

AMB
12th November 2019

PART 1
THEORY

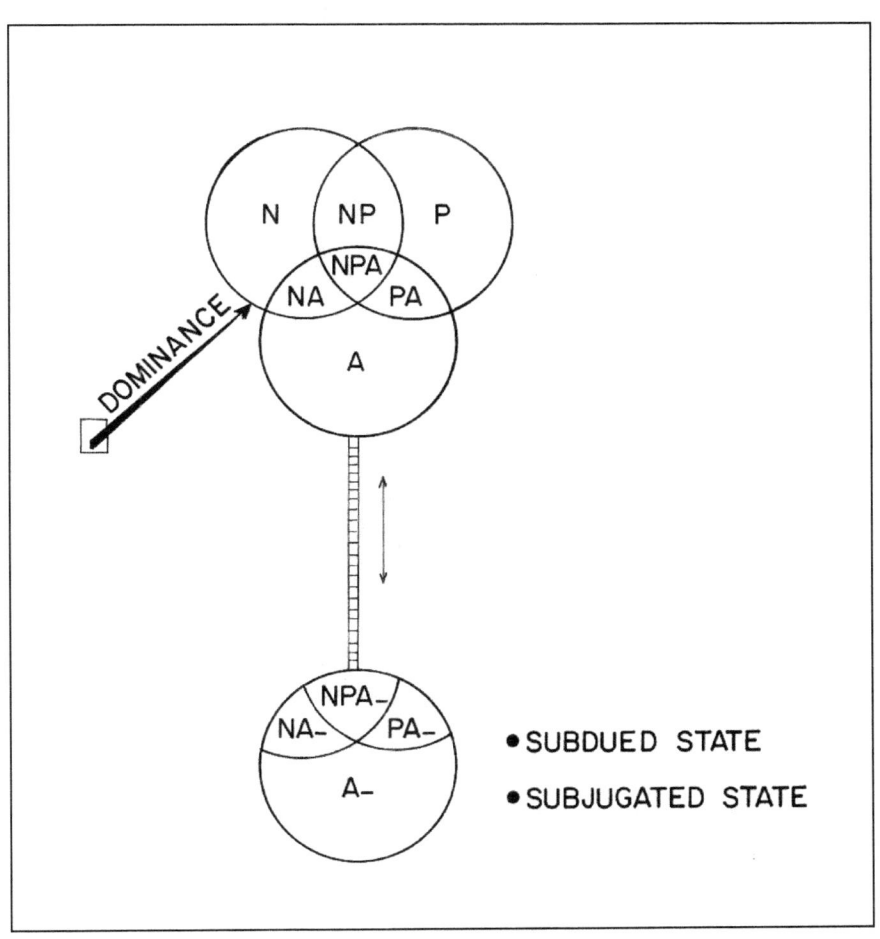

1 **Venn diagram of NPA types: dominance and submission.**

Character types having the trait of aggression
A may change, reversibly, to a subdued or
subjugated state, A−.

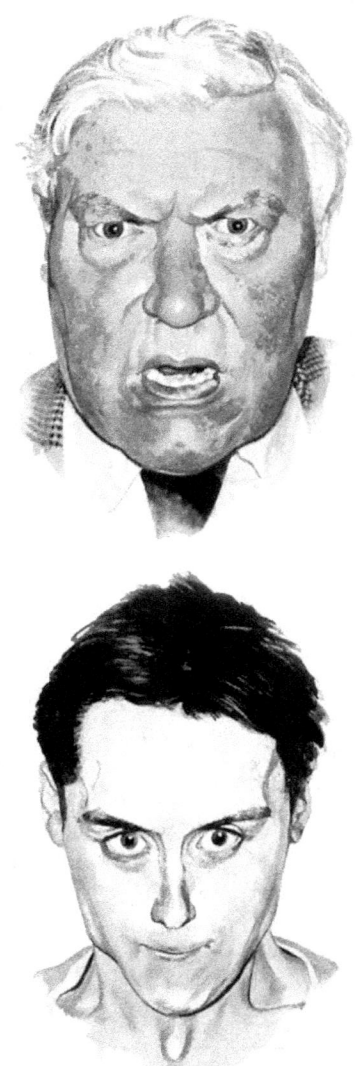

2   Faces in rage: the N and A rages.

Pictured are sanguine and non-sanguine types.

In sanguine individuals having both the N and A traits, the two rages may be expressed together as an "NA rage".

[*Anthony Moore*]

3 Character types according to the ancient theory of humors:
Phlegmaticus, Cholericus, Sanguineus and *Melancholicus.*

The concept that humans have identifiable personality
types goes back at least to Hippocrates, or *ca.* 400 B.C.

[*J.K. Lavater, ca. 1775*]

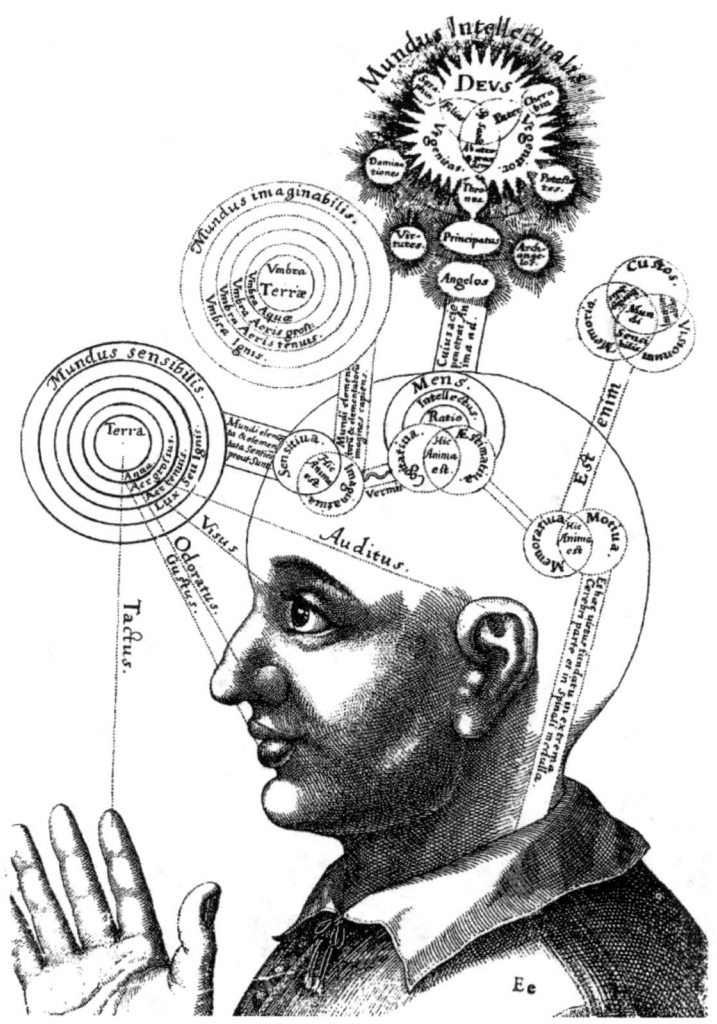

4   **The Mind of the Microcosm, from Robert Fludd's**
Utriusque Cosmi Historia, **1619.**

Fludd was an English physician who embarked on
the ambitious project of surveying all the human
knowledge available at his time.

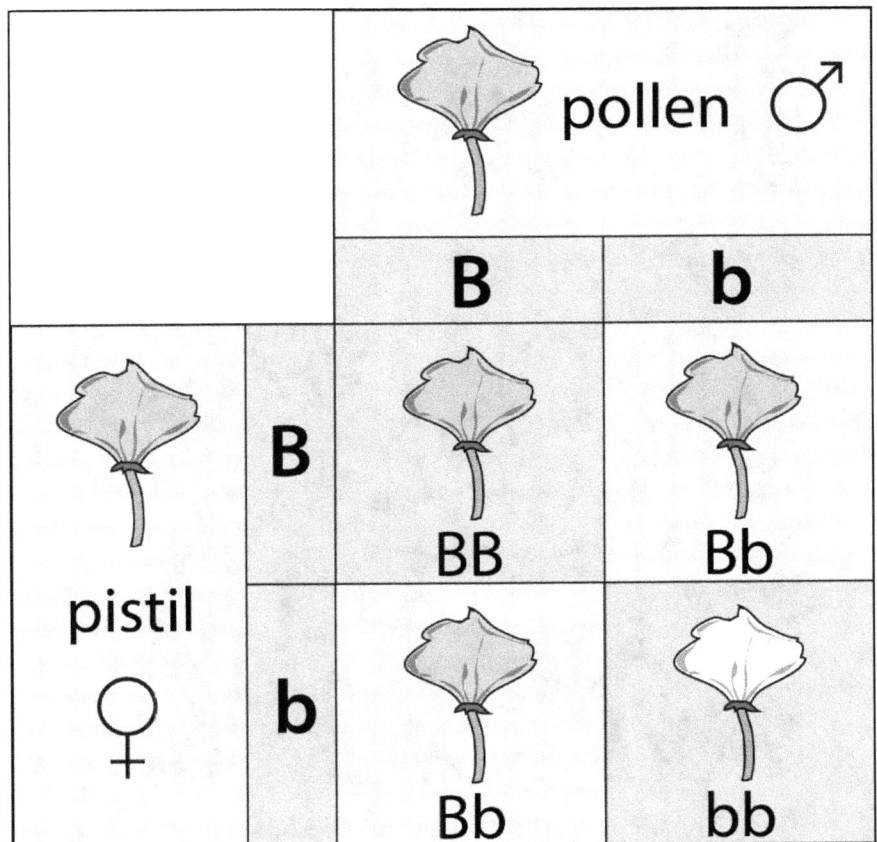

5   **The Punnett Square: a visual representation of Mendelian inheritance.**

The diagram shows, for a flower, a male-female cross for a single gene having dominant and recessive alleles.

In the NPA model, the situation is more complicated: there is assortment of three separate genes, corresponding to the traits N, P and A.

[*Andrea Laurel*]

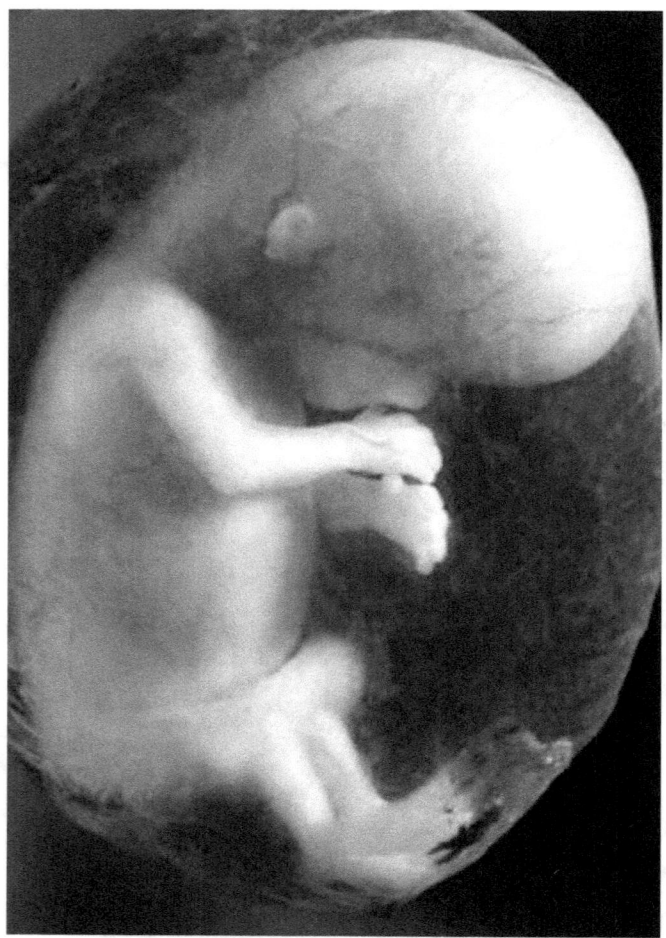

6 **"The die is cast": the basis of personality is genetic.**

There are many environmental aspects to personality and behavior. Nevertheless, the basic structure of personality: one's gender and the NPA traits, is determined at conception.

[Kambodza]

	N	A	NP	NA	PA	NPA
N	N -- -- NA -- -- -- --	"	"	"	"	"
A	N -- -- NA -- -- 0 A	-- -- -- NA -- -- -- A	"	"	"	"
NP	N NP -- NA NPA -- -- --	N NP P NA NPA PA 0 A	N NP -- NA NPA -- -- --	"	"	"
NA	N -- -- NA -- -- -- --	-- -- -- NA -- -- -- A	N NP -- NA NPA -- -- --	-- -- -- NA -- -- -- --	"	"
PA	N NP P NA NPA PA 0 A	-- -- -- NA NPA PA -- A	N NP P NA NPA PA 0 A	-- -- -- NA NPA PA -- A	-- -- -- NA NPA PA -- A	"
NPA	N NP -- NA NPA -- -- --	-- -- -- NA NPA PA -- A	N NP -- NA NPA -- -- --	-- -- -- NA NPA -- -- --	-- -- -- NA NPA PA -- A	-- -- -- NA NPA -- -- --
FATHER OR MOTHER	N	A	NP	NA	PA	NPA

7   Progeny Chart: possible NPA types of offspring.

The P and null (0) types in the encircled areas are non-viable. They would result in miscarriage, stillbirth or an infant who fails to thrive.

For example, a parental match NPA×PA could result in children only of type NA, NPA, PA or A, with no non-viable conceptions.

In contrast, parental matches such as N×A or N×PA could be infertile, the result of non-viable P or null types in the progeny.

THE ENIGMA OF SHORT PARENTS WHO HAVE TALL CHILDREN

8   The basis of physical stature, like that of personality, is mostly genetic.

According to the NPA model, personality type and physical stature are genetically linked in some families.

Tall children in a family where the parents are short can be due to a pair of *complementary genes* inherited from the parents, one from the father and one from the mother.

Sometimes, two parents who are both of short stature will have all children — no matter how many — who are considerably taller.

9 **A tall bridal couple with short parents.**

If the couple have children, how tall will they be?

The NPA model can be used to predict the likelihood of tall children in some families where height is closely linked to the NP personality type.

[*Katherine Hala*]

10   **A tall NP type and a short A type: Abraham Lincoln (6'4"/193 cm) and Vladimir Putin (5'6"/168 cm).**

The NP and the A types are "mirror images" of each other, in the sense that neither has any of the NPA traits of the other.

The frequent occurrences of tall NP types and short A types suggest a genetic link between personality type and stature.

[*Bill Oberst Jr.*]

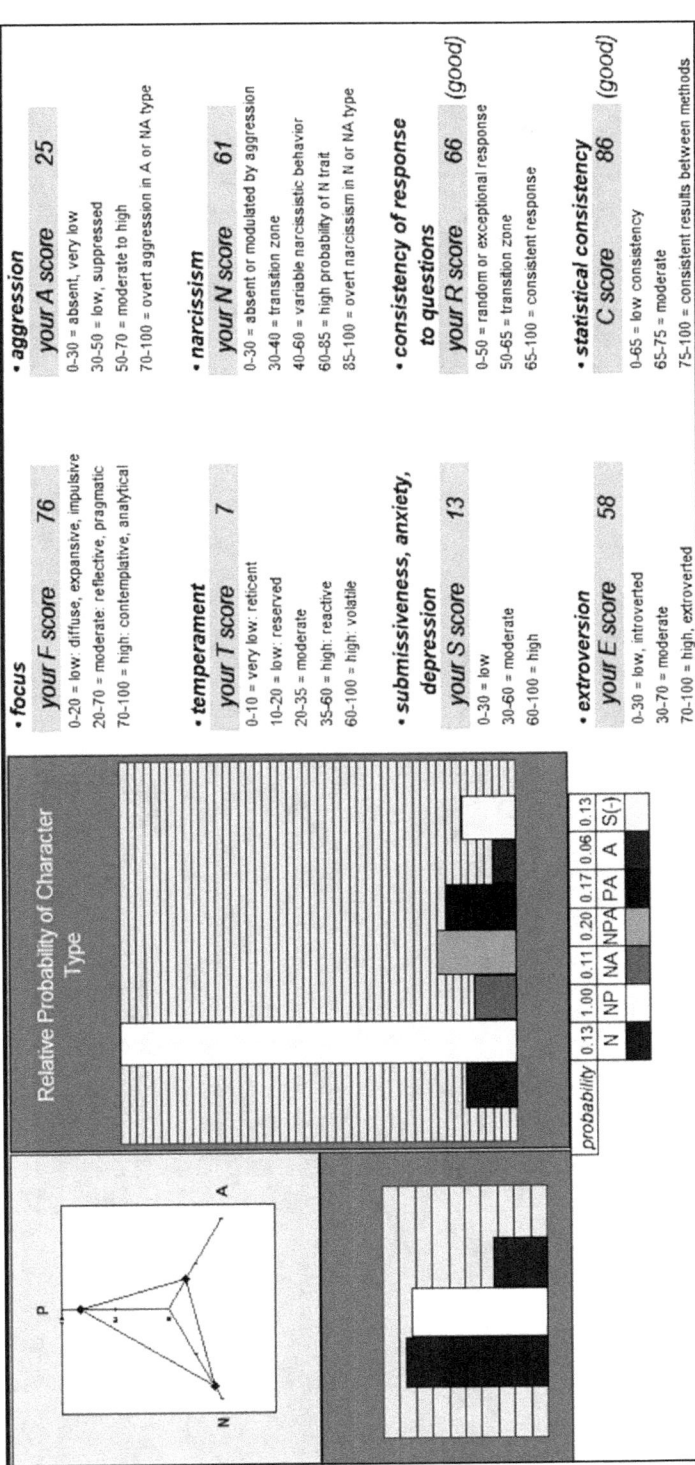

• focus
your F score   76
0-20 = low: diffuse, expansive, impulsive
20-70 = moderate: reflective, pragmatic
70-100 = high: contemplative, analytical

• temperament
your T score   7
0-10 = very low: reticent
10-20 = low: reserved
20-35 = moderate
35-60 = high: reactive
60-100 = high: volatile

• submissiveness, anxiety, depression
your S score   13
0-30 = low
30-60 = moderate
60-100 = high

• extroversion
your E score   58
0-30 = low, introverted
30-70 = moderate
70-100 = high, extroverted

• aggression
your A score   25
0-30 = absent, very low
30-50 = low, suppressed
50-70 = moderate to high
70-100 = overt aggression in A or NA type

• narcissism
your N score   61
0-30 = absent or modulated by aggression
30-40 = transition zone
40-60 = variable narcissistic behavior
60-85 = high probability of N trait
85-100 = overt narcissism in N or NA type

• consistency of response to questions
your R score   66   (good)
0-50 = random or exceptional response
50-65 = transition zone
65-100 = consistent response

• statistical consistency
your C score   86   (good)
0-65 = low consistency
65-75 = moderate
75-100 = consistent results between methods

Relative Probability of Character Type

probability	0.13	1.00	0.11	0.20	0.17	0.06	0.13
	N	NP	NA	NPA	PA	A	S(-)

11 NPA personality test: computer display. The bar graphs show the relative probabilities of the three NPA traits (*left*) and types (*right*). The subject was male, age 31 to 40 years and the parent of an autistic child. The results indicate an NP type with a low S score of 13.

PART 2

SANGUINITY: THE N TRAIT

12   **Gingival smile of the N trait: It's all about recognition.**

The meaning of the smile of sanguinity is not
joy, but rather: "I recognize you and
acknowledge your appreciation of me."

[*Max Thinks Sees*]

13   Response to recognition: a smile, arm gestures and a curtsy.

Smiling, bowing, curtsying and expansive arm gestures are instinctive expressions of social contact associated with the N trait.

[*Canhasal*]

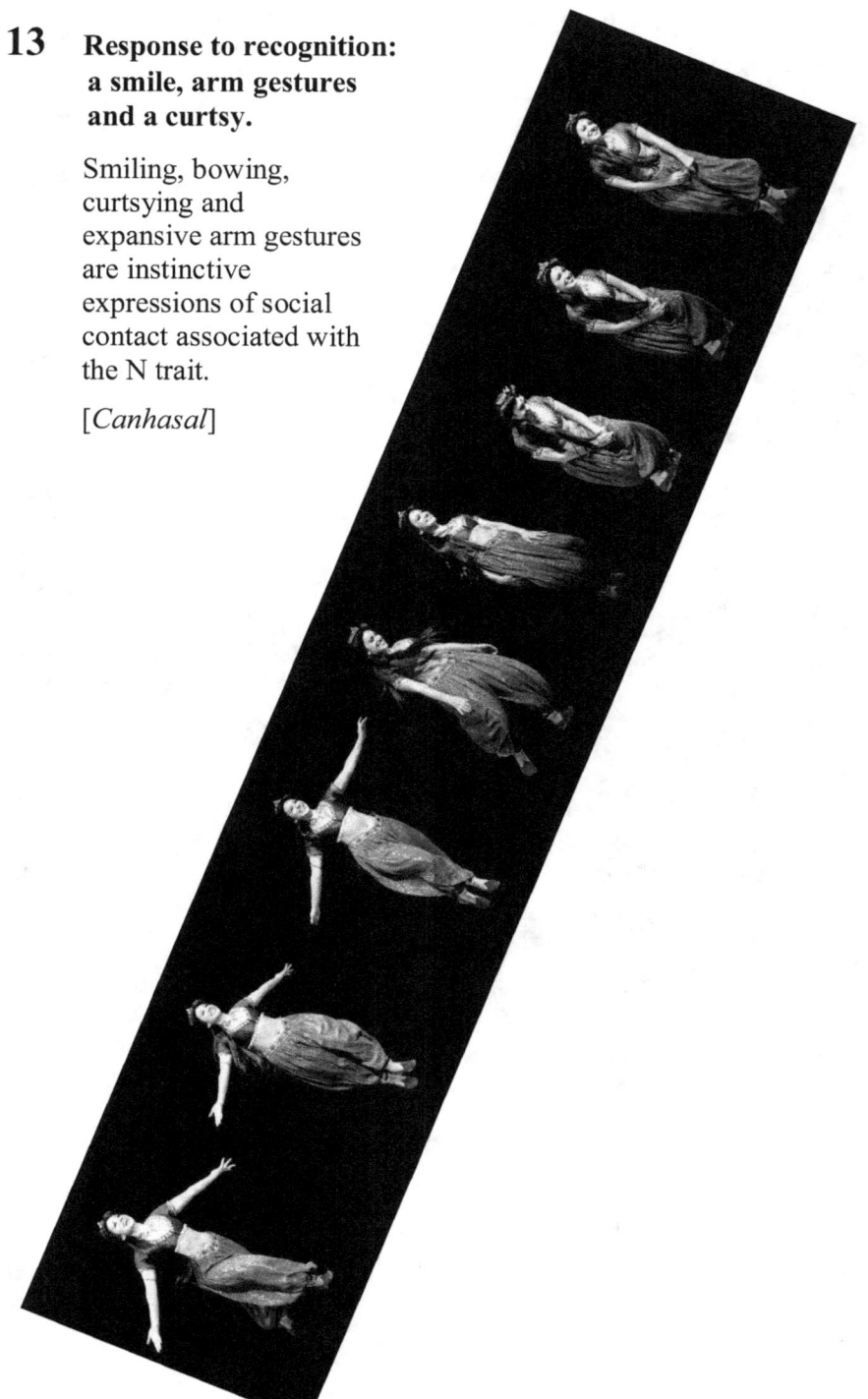

14   **Greeting a friend: an instinctive smile of recognition.**

In contrast, smiling to a stranger, or excessively to
an audience, can be interpreted as "narcissistic",
with the meaning "Even though you don't know
me, I bestow recognition onto you as the most
wonderful (or talented) person that I am!"

[*Matthew Kenwrick*]

15   Gestures of the N trait: the Narcissistic Arms Pose.

Its meaning is "I embrace your recognition of me as the wonderful person that I am!" or simply… "I'm the greatest!"

[*Mihai Paraschiv*]

16   **Gestures of the N trait: a child shows an instinctive pose of recognition.**

In individuals having the N trait, social smiling and expansive arm gestures are innate and begin at an early age.

17   **Gestures of the N trait: the Joan of Arc Pose.**

When confronted with an expansive vista, an individual may exhibit the "narcissistic arms pose" with an upward gaze.

Although the person is alone, the pose is identical to that of acknowledging applause before a large audience.

The quasi-religious meaning is: "May the heavens above recognize me for the most wonderful person that I am!"

[*Lucas Mohamd*]

18   **Gestures of the N trait: Hallelujah!**

Here, the elevated gaze and expansive arm gesture occur spontaneously in a religious setting.

[*House of Praise*]

19   Gestures of the N trait: a smile by another name.

In a shy individual who has difficulty smiling for the camera, the "narcissistic arms pose" can appear as the replacement for a smile.

Here, writer Somerset Maugham demonstrates the gesture.

[*Rank Organisation*]

20   **The sanguine "selfie": It's all about me!**

Self-admiration in a mirror or the taking of
excessive photos of oneself can be related to the
narcissistic aspects of the N trait.

[*H.G. Bäckman*]

21 **Signs of the N trait: blushing.**

Blushing or flushing occurs most easily in sanguine
individuals. The NP type is especially prone to
blushing with embarrassment.

[*Anne-Lise Heinrichs*]

22 **Signs of the N trait: tearfulness.**

A propensity to tearfulness is more common in the sanguine types.

Above, Paris on June 14, 1940.

[*Flickr*]

23   **The N trait: tattoo exhibitionism.**

Like other extravagant adornment, the flaunting of elaborate tattoos can be related to the narcissistic aspects of the N trait.

[*Pexels UK*]

←

24   **The N trait: "showing off" exhibitionism.**

Extravagant behavior whose purpose is to draw attention to oneself is all the more alluring if it is dangerous.

At left, a Filipino boy does acrobatics in a park.

[*T.C. Manasan*]

25 **Narcissus!**

When not modulated by the P trait, the N trait is often expressed as "narcissism".

The term comes from Narcissus, the figure of Greek mythology who became enraptured by his own reflected image.

[*H.T. McLin*]

26 **Showtime! The glamorous extravaganza.**

Here, we see the ultimate in unbridled narcissistic display: bright colors, smiling, dancing, expansive arm gestures and loud bombastic music.

[*Adam Taylor*]

PART 3

PERFECTIONISM: THE P TRAIT

27   **P trait: Florence Cathedral.**

Hallmarks of the P trait are neatness, order, symmetry, repetition and attention to detail. The trait is evident where there is a high prevalence of NP types, as in northern Italy.

[*Lee Herrera*]

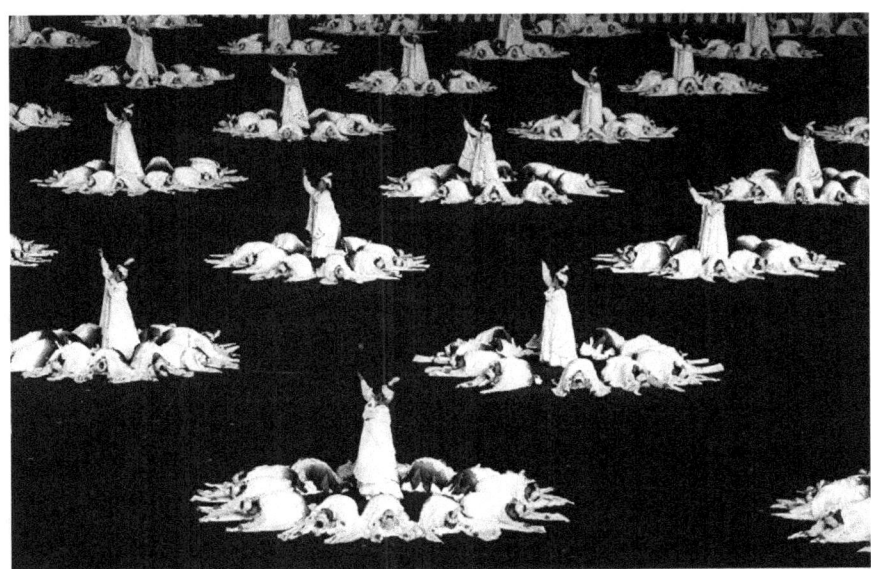

28 **P trait: Korean gymnastics festival.**

Here, the trait of perfectionism is much in evidence. Koreans are mostly a mix of N and NP types, but the NP types are clearly in charge here.

[*Laika*]

←

29 **P trait: Terracotta Army.**

Some of the more than 8,000 life-size, individually sculptured warriors guarding the tomb of Emperor Qin Shi Huang Di (Xi'an, China). Like Korea, much of north and central China has a high prevalence of perfectionistic NP types.

[*Richard Fisher*]

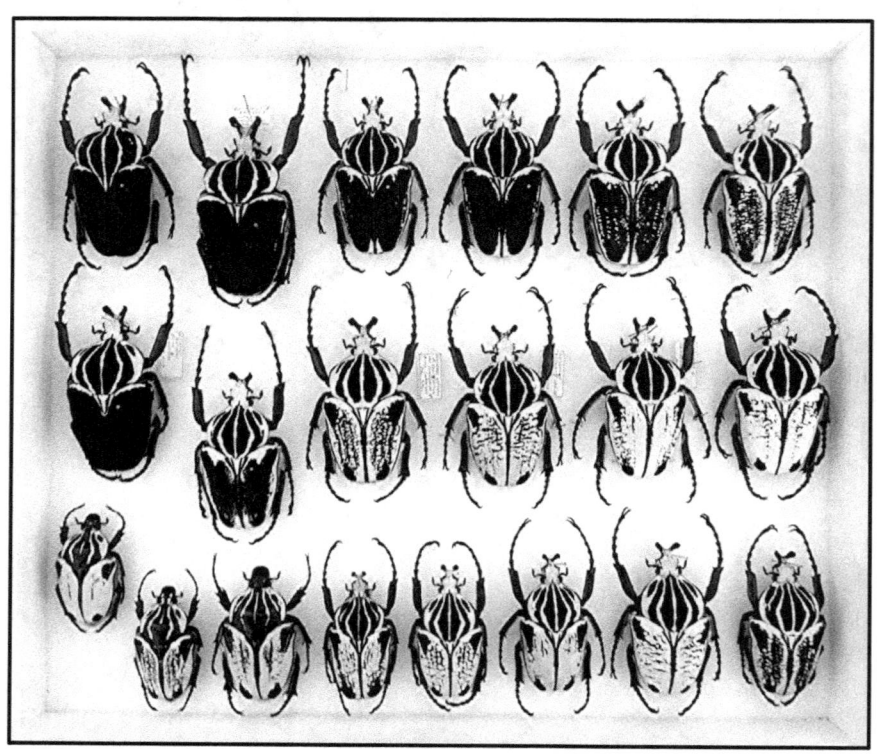

30   **P trait: beetle collection.**

Here we see all aspects of the P trait:
neatness, order, symmetry, repetition
and attention to detail.

[*Justin Sewell*]

31 **Presence and absence of P trait in music.**

Top: Perfectionism in music, as depicted in a medieval liturgical manuscript.

[*Grant Barclay*]

Bottom: Non-perfectionistic music, as exemplified by jazz. Shown are Buddy Childers with Stan Kenton on the trumpet.

[*W.P. Gottlieb*]

32   P trait: surgical masks in public.

Scrupulous attention to cleanliness and hygiene is most often found in perfectionistic types. Like Korea, Japan has a high prevalence of NP types, who are sometimes denigrated as being overly "obsessive-compulsive".

[*Matthew Kenwrick*]

←

33   K-pop: the N and P traits together.

Put N and NP types together, and the result is K-pop music.

[*Republic of Korea*]

34   P trait: black rectangular eyeglasses.

The NP type, in particular, has a liking for this conservative brand of eyewear.

In general, the restrained NP type has an aversion to colorful display and to lack of symmetry.

[*Igor Link*]

35 **Absence of P trait: colorful apparel with non-symmetric pattern.**

The non-perfectionistic NA type is especially attracted to uncoordinated colors and multi-colored flair.

[*Min An*]

PART 4

AGGRESSION: THE A TRAIT

36   **Trait A: non-sanguine aggression.**

In Iran, a respected authoritarian figure is known for his non-sanguine complexion, strong eye contact, lack of smile and uncompromising demeanor.

[*Humbleslave*]

37   Trait A: non-sanguine grins and laughs.

Non-sanguine types do not have the capacity to exhibit the gingival social smile. Above: examples of facial expressions in non-sanguine A and PA types that are sometimes interpreted as social smiling.

[*Patricia Moss-Vreeland*]

38   Gestures of the A trait: the intimidating glare.

"... What are you looking at?"

    [*Fredrik Lindström*]

↓ 39   Gestures of the A trait: the aggressive finger point.

Often accompanied by the intimidating glare,
the meaning is "One false move and you are
under attack!"

[*Alex Berger*]

40   **The eye contact of dominance and submission.**

Top: Peter the Great interrogates his doomed son, Alexei. [*Tretyakov Gallery*]

Bottom: Always nervous in social situations, an aspiring Adolf Hitler avoids eye contact with President von Hindenburg, 1933. [*Bundesarchiv*]

41   Gestures of the A trait: the clenched fist.

In types having the A trait, the clenched fist is often an instinctive response.

Although usually displayed in the context of a threat, it can also be displayed as a greeting.

[*David Goehring*]

42   **A confrontational pose of aggression: Rapper Ludacris.**

The meaning of the gesture is clear: "You're
welcome to mess with me... but at your own risk!"

[*Intel Free Press*]

43   Gestures of the A trait: the choke.

The gesture has the meaning: "The end is nigh!"

It can be used as a threat, or as Vladimir Putin demonstrates, a playful expression of vulnerability.

[*M. Metzel*]

44   Violence!

Incidents of violence are most often related to the trait of aggression, for example if there are challenges within a "pecking order". However, violence may also be based on the N trait, especially on occasions of wounded vanity.

[*Apionid*]

45 **When non-sanguine meets sanguine: the non-sanguine "selfie".**

Russian cosmonaut Fyodor Yurchikhin patiently tolerates the exhortations of sanguine visitors to be photogenic.

[*Alexander Vysotsky*]

46 **When sanguine meets non-sanguine: espousal in Latvia.**

Non-sanguinity is prevalent in Eastern Europe, and it is not uncommon for intermarriage to occur between sanguine and non-sanguine types, as in the couples depicted at left.

[*Rolands Lakis & Konstantin Lazorkin*]

47   When the N and A traits come together: the NA type.

In the NA type, both the N and A traits are fully expressed, without modulation by the P trait. The result is often an individual where "unbridled" narcissism and aggression are overtly evident.

Above, comedienne Joan Rivers.

[*Flickr*]

48   **When the N, P and A traits all come together: the NPA type.**

In the NPA Dominant type, the N and A traits are fully expressed, however with modulation by the P trait.

The result is sometimes a highly extroverted "managerial-autocratic" personality who demands "spit and polish".

Above, General Norman Schwarzkopf.

[*U.A Army*]

PART 5

INHIBITION OF AGGRESSION: PASSIVE AGGRESSIVE TYPES

49 **Shyness in a child.**

Shyness is a condition often related to genetic inhibition of the A trait ("A− trait").

As the condition is inherited, it can be discerned at an early age.

[*Poonam Agarwal*]

50   **Camera-shy.**

Passive Aggressive types having the A− trait can
be very camera averse, even to the point of its
being a phobia.

[*Isthmene Yoshizawa*]

51 Camera aversion.

An introverted individual may use a prop to avoid eye contact with the camera.

Here, writer Somerset Maugham demonstrates.

[*Rank Organisation*]

52   **Camera aversion: "mugging for the camera".**

Shy individuals may exhibit exaggerated facial expressions and gestures to hide their discomfort before the camera lens.

[*Julie Laurent*]

53   **Stage fright.**

Aversion to public speaking, often to the point of
its being a phobia, is common in Passive
Aggressive types having the A− trait.

[*Neil Moralee*]

PART 6

INVERSIONS:
PSEUDO-AGGRESSION AND
PSEUDO-NARCISSISM

Flexgraph.fr
Photo Graph

54   **Pseudo-aggression: the Goth girl.**

The Goth style is an inversion of sanguinity, with a disdain for smiling, bright colors and extroverted display. In an N type, the result is someone who can resemble an austere, non-sanguine PA individual.

55   Pseudo-narcissism: adornment in a non-sanguine type.

When a PA type exhibits adornment, as in the tattooed individual above, the result can superficially resemble the display of sanguinity.

Above, "Industrial Girl" from Latvia.

[*Konstantin Lazorkin*]

56   **Pseudo-narcissism: Boy George, then and now.**

As a non-sanguine type, the singer's former androgynous appearance and current punky adornment have aspects that superficially resemble narcissistic display of the N trait.

[D. Stockings]

PART 7

CARICATURES OF
THE CHARACTER TYPES

57   **N type: the glory seeker.**

The portrayal here is Barack Obama as a charismatic individual having the classical gingival smile of sanguinity.

[*DonkeyHotey*]

58   N type: "Princess".

The N princess is depicted as a glamorous, non-perfectionistic, needy individual. Of course, the lipstick is red in color, and copious.

[*Swallows Gallery*]

59   NA type: the *prima donna*.

"... *I said I want it, and I want it now!*"

[*SilviaP Design*]

60   **N type: the flighty space cadet.**

"Don't bother me with details…"
"Whatever…."

[Isra Garcia]

61   **N type: Lady in red.**

Red is the darling color of the N type, especially in clothing and especially in the female.

Wherever N types congregate — irrespective of ethnicity — one can be sure that the color red will be displayed prominently.

[*June Yarham*]

62   NA type: Lady with pink hair.

The favorite color of the NA type is usually *not* red. He or she goes for pink, yellow, orange… even chartreuse. And sometimes all of them together in a multi-colored mélange.

[*Lauren Gledhill*]

63   **NA type: the scandalmonger.**

She will revel in the intimate details of the affairs of others… as well as her own.

In her own mind, she is saucy, sexy, sensuous and seductive.

A vampire in her dreams.

[*Katy & George UK*]

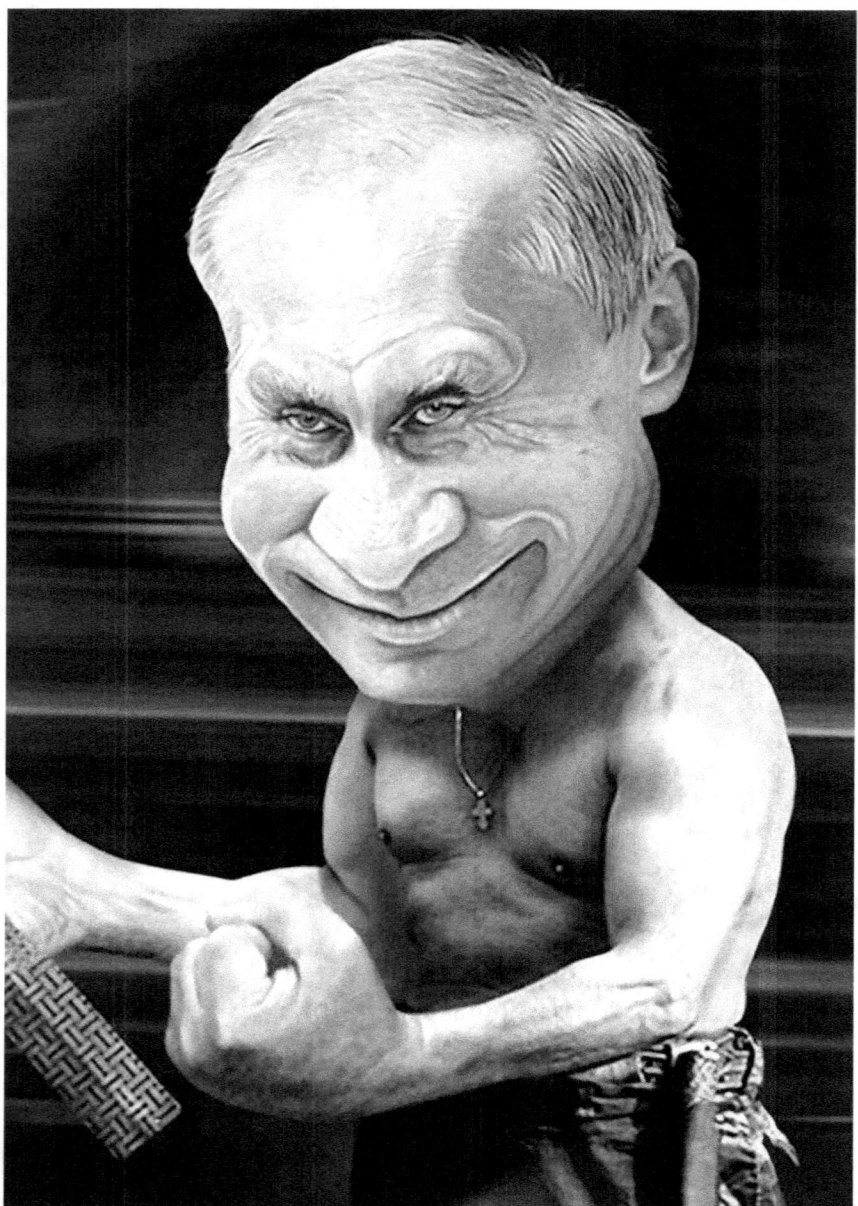

64   A type: the arrogant dynamo.

Vladimir Putin, exhibiting the clenched fist of aggression, is caricaturized as a non-sanguine individual who stands for strength and defiance.

[*DonkeyHotey*]

65 **An A type with "short man syndrome".**

Short in stature, wiry, with a pallid complexion and an odd grimace instead of a smile, the non-perfectionistic, pugnacious "A type" pays little attention to matters of style or physical appearance.

[*Ryan McGuire*]

66   **NP type: the phlegmatic-melancholic personality.**

Angela Merkel is caricaturized as a sanguine,
serious, somewhat homely individual, devoid of
charisma.

[*DonkeyHotey*]

67 **NP type with "tall man syndrome".**

Obsessive and compulsive, ruminating and melancholic, the non-aggressive NP type contemplates his next move with care.

Characteristics often seen in the NP type of European heritage are tall stature, an oval face, and a tendency to premature baldness.

[*Szilárd Szabó*]

68   PA type: the "Power behind the throne".

The portrayal here is Richard Cheney as a non-sanguine, Machiavellian individual showing a sneer, rather than the warm smile of sanguinity.

[*DonkeyHotey*]

69   **Eastern European PA type.**

Haughty and sometimes fierce, she is pure perfectionistic aggression. The complexion is milky white. She would not dream of using red lipstick.

[*Pixabay*]

70   PA type: the false smiler.

In an effort to show a friendly countenance to bolster a forced smile, the eyebrows are raised and the brow is furrowed. The resulting intense facial expression mimics the sanguine smile. Above, First Lady Nancy Reagan demonstrates.

[*Flickr*]

71 **PA type: the Robert Mitchum look.**

Here, only one eyebrow is raised with a furrowed brow, and there is little attempt at a smile. It is a subtle facial expression of recognition in a non-sanguine type.

[*Wikipedia*]

72 **NPA Dominant type: the managerial-autocratic personality.**

A heavyweight in the personality department, with all three
NPA traits fully expressed, Christopher Christie is portrayed at
the podium as a sanguine, bossy personage.

[*DonkeyHotey*]

73 **NPA Dominant type: the virago.**

Never at a loss for words, the sanguine,
overbearing Queen of Hearts from "Alice in
Wonderland" makes a point.

[*John Tenniel*]

74   NPA Dominant type: the matron.

Known for her forceful voice and commanding
demeanor, she puts up with nonsense from
nobody.

[*Simon Cliff*]

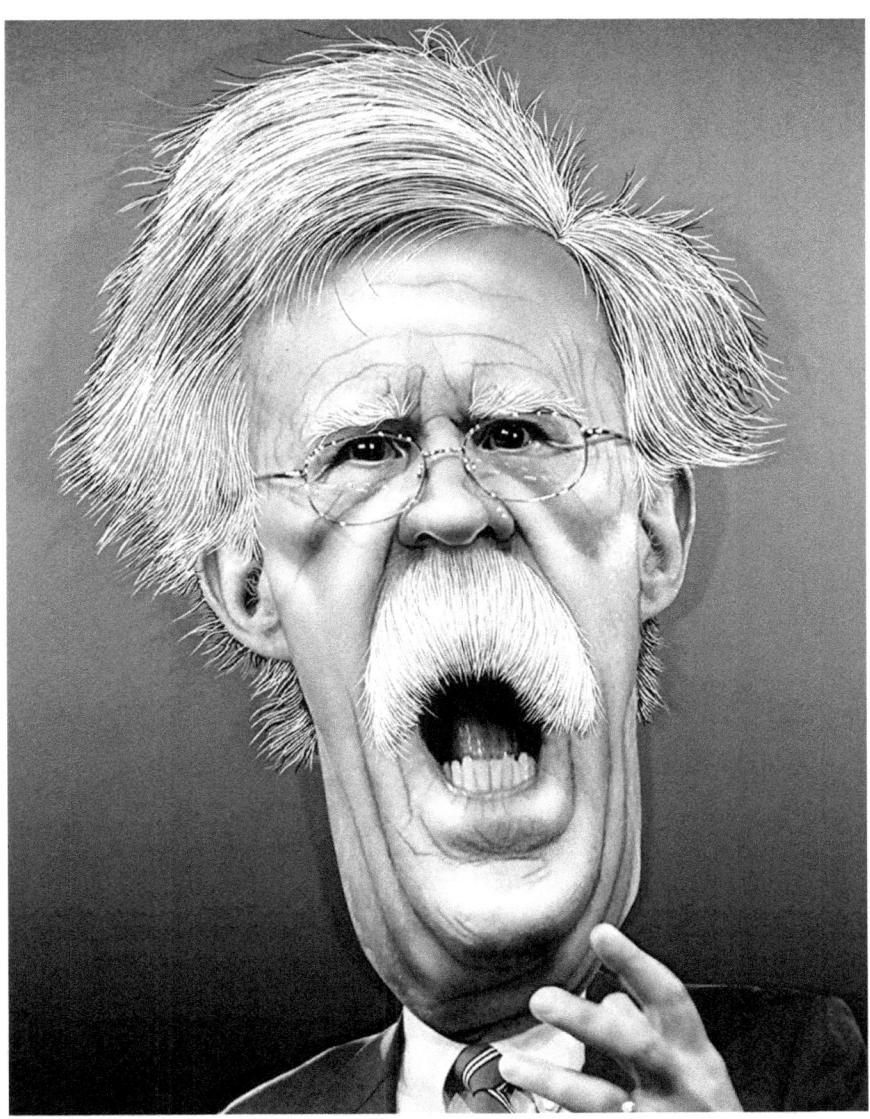

75   **NPA Dominant type: the sanguine warmonger.**

Above, national security advisor John Bolton,
for whom any international disagreement not
leading to war is a missed opportunity.

[*DonkeyHotey*]

76   **Pseudo non-sanguine type: the forlorn N type.**

In times of trouble, the sanguine smile of sociability is nowhere to be seem.

Above, Sioux Chief Phizi Gall, who routed Custer and corps at Little Bighorn in 1876, pictured after his eventual abdication.

[*David Frances Barry*]

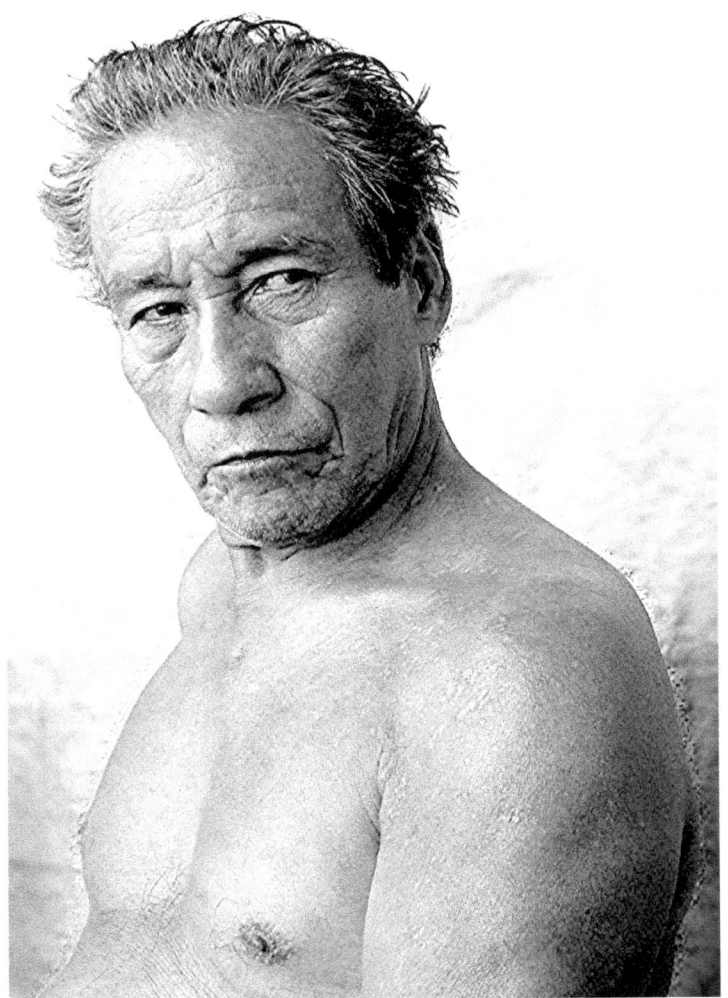

77   **Pseudo non-sanguine type: the antagonized NPA Dominant type.**

"Who the hell are you… and who said that I wanted my picture taken?"

Although usually sociable and gregarious, he does not like to have his space invaded, and he certainly does not suffer fools gladly. Here, he may be on the brink of an explosive "NA rage".

[*Mayeli Espinosa Rios*]

78   NA type: the zany comic.

Jerry Lewis is portrayed as the hyperactive, charismatic, larger-than-life comedian that he was.

[*Dean Huck*]

79   PA type: the non-sanguine sardonic wit.

Bill Maher, the political commentator and comedian,
is depicted as an acerbic, pallid individual with a
facial expression that is more a mocking snicker than
a social smile.

[*DonkeyHotey*]

80   NP type: the cerebral Vulcan.

In the fictional series, *Star Trek*, Vulcans are characterized by rigid, logical reasoning and a stunted capacity for displaying emotions.

Above, Mr. Spock (played by NP actor, Leonard Nimoy) displays the Vulcan salute.

[*Roberto Rizzato*]

81 N type: the showgirl.

More important than the song and dance is having an elegant physique and a flair for stylish exhibitionism in scanty attire.

Above, Josephine Baker, "the Black Venus", iconic vaudeville performer of the 1920's.

[*Pixabay*]

82   **N type: the possessive paramour.**

"I will NOT be ignored...!"

She can be a *femme fatale...* in the
literal sense of the term.

[*Oliana Gruzdeva*]

83   **The con artist: N and NA types.**

Whether they be deceiving smooth talkers or insistent blowhards, con artists come in two basic varieties: those who wish to advance their career or social status… and those who wish to separate you from your money.

[*Sue Cro*]

84   **NA type: the playboy.**

With immense vitality, and incapable of
being embarrassed, he leaves a long trail
of jilted lovers in his wake.

[*Amy Z*]

85 NA type: the girthy sexpot.

Yes, she knows that she is overweight, and she knows that she is a vamp, but that is what she is, and she is proud of it.

[*Flickr*]

86   NP type: the middle-aged puritan.

"Sex?? You're kidding? I've already had my children...
I don't need it, and I certainly don't want it!"

[Pexels UK]

87   **NPA− Passive Aggressive type: the agitated achiever.**

Elizabeth Warren is caricaturized as a hyperactive, vulnerable individual.

The notation "A−" signifies partial inhibition of trait A having a genetic basis.

[*DonkeyHotey*]

88   NPA– Passive Aggressive type: the introverted workaholic.

Prime Minister Modi of India is portrayed as a reserved,
somewhat melancholic individual, who is nevertheless
always ready to rise to the occasion and verbally skewer
his opponents.

[*DonkeyHotey*]

89 NA− **Passive Aggressive type: the sensitive aesthete.**

Michael Jackson is portrayed as a vulnerable
individual: an unfathomable combination of talent,
unbridled narcissism and inhibited aggression.

[*Wikipedia*]

90   **NPA= Passive Aggressive type: the submissive scholar.**

The portrayal of Charles Darwin is that of an introverted, camera-shy individual. A social phobia prevented him from presenting in public his monumental work on evolution.

The notation "A=" signifies profound inhibition of trait A having a genetic basis.

[*Wikipedia*]

91   **NA= Passive Aggressive type: the battered woman.**

Those most vulnerable to spousal abuse, be they male or female, are submissive individuals with the A− or A= trait.

[*Flickr*]

92 **Resigned type NP–A: the recluse.**

"...It needs a good deal of philosophy not to be mortified by the thought of persons who have voluntarily abandoned everything that for the most of us makes life worth living and are devoid of envy of what they have missed. I have never made up my mind whether they are fools or wise men. They have given up everything for a dream, a dream of peace or happiness or freedom, and their dream is so intense that they make it true." — W.S. Maugham, *The Gentleman in the Parlour*, 1930. [*N. Mladjenovic*]

←

93 **Resigned types.**

The Resigned type is a mature individual who has given up "playing the game" of dominance and submission, and has adopted a lifestyle of splendid independence.

Here, individuals in a library are pictured as solitary souls who have no desire to become involved in the complications of social interaction. [*Greg Nissen*]

PART 8

HISTORICAL FIGURES

94 **Napoleon Bonaparte: N type.**

Somewhat paunchy in his later years, the Emperor was a sanguine individual who had the capacity of a smile "that would light up his entire countenance".

[*National Gallery of Art*]

95   Abraham Lincoln: NP type.

Tall and lean, strong and stubborn, with impeccable handwriting, the 16th president remains the quintessential male American NP type.

[*Chicago Historical Society*]

96 **Mary Lincoln: NA type.**

A somewhat inappropriate match to her NP husband, Mary was known for her high spirits and hysterical outbursts.

[*Library of Congress*]

97   Henry VIII: N type.

"Bluff King Hal" was known for his charismatic
effrontery… and his difficulties with women.

[*Thyssen-Bornemisza Collection*]

98   **Katherine of Aragon: NP type.**

Somewhat stodgy and lacking flair, the first wife of Henry VIII was known for her virtue, piety, dignity and level-headedness. She stood up to Henry's bullying with uncompromising stubbornness.

[*Kunsthistorisches Museum*]

99   **Charles I and Cardinal Richelieu: perfectionist types.**

Character traits can sometimes be read from an individual's countenance. The effect of the P trait in introverted sanguine types is toward an appearance of seriousness, reserve and melancholy.

[*Courtesy of H.M. the Queen & the National Gallery*]

100 **Friedrich Wilhelm I: NPA type.**

With all three NPA traits fully expressed, the portly, pedantic father of Frederick the Great was known for his autocratic demeanor and explosive rages.

[*Schloss Charlottenburg*]

101 **Rasputin: NA type.**

The profligacy of the hyperactive mystic from Siberia was legendary. Seductive and charismatic, he was known to wear pink or bright yellow shirts.

A nervous individual, he was always fussing with his hair and beard.

[*Imperial War Museum*]

102   **Joseph Stalin: A type.**

A non-sanguine aggressive type who achieved absolute power, which then corrupted him… absolutely.

Shown here demonstrating the "aggressive finger point", Stalin was ruthless and brutal, even to his family.

[Archival image]

103   **Adolf Hitler: a Passive Aggressive NPA− type.**

Although Hitler's policies were characteristic of
unbridled aggression, as a private individual he was
a socially inept, repressed aggressive personage,
very unlike his demeanor on the podium.

[*Flickr*]

104   Jesus Christ.

Since everyone agrees that the famous religious figures of the past were mortal humans, theologians will eventually agree that they had specific NPA personality types.

[*Joseph Wallace King*]

PART 9

COUPLES

105   NP×NP type: "American Gothic".

Above, Grant Wood's iconic portrait of two
individuals from the American heartland, mid-
twentieth century.

106 N×PA type: sanguine and non-sanguine partners.

Seemingly poles apart, these two individuals often find each other.

The N and PA types may be considered to be "mirror images", in the sense that neither has any of the NPA traits of the other.

[*Oliana Gruzdeva*]

107 Weddings: Jewish (NPA×NPA) and Bulgarian Christian (NP×NP).

Top: The groom speaks in a forceful voice heard clearly in all four corners of the temple. The Ashkenazi are typically sanguine, and the NPA Dominant type is common.

[*Krista Guenin*]

Bottom: Nearing the end of two-day festivities, the good-natured NP groom has patiently tolerated all manner of traditional custom.

[*Rosendr*]

108   N×N type: a same-sex relationship.

Due to "other genes" and environment, there can be a
diversity in a particular NPA type, as depicted above.
(See also Plate 54.)

[Ashley Webb]

109   **A×N type: pure A and N traits come together.**

Sometimes opposites attract.

Above, Roman Polanski and Sharon Tate in 1968.

[*J. Garofalo*]

110 NA×NA type: a non-perfectionistic relationship.

Characterized by unbridled narcissism and aggression, this can be a labile liaison, indeed.

The NA type is the only one that always "breeds true": all children of any two NA types must be NA types as well.

[*F. Cordoba*]

111 Comedy duos: Laurel & Hardy (N×NPA) and The Honeymooners (NPA×NPA).

Top: The timorous Stan Laurel is paired with the bombastic Oliver Hardy.

Bottom: As Dominant NPA types, Jackie Gleason and Audrey Meadows were an even match.

Other twentieth century comedy teams included Burns & Allen (N×N), Abbott & Costello (A×NA), and Martin & Lewis (N×NA).

112   NA×NPA− type: the "game" of dominance & submission.

Very different indeed, the extroverted NA type and the restrained NPA− type seem destined to act out love-hate intimacy having abundant fireworks but little stability.

[*Nathan Dumlao*]

113   A×NPA− type: the King of Siam and Anna.

In the film version, the king (Yul Brynner) is cast as an authoritarian A type, while the prim Anna (Deborah Kerr) plays the role of a not-always-submissive NPA− type.

[*Capitol Records*]

114   Identical twins: identical NPA type.

It is common knowledge that identical twins — even those raised apart — have similar personalities… a subtle proof that the human personality has genetic origins.

Above, folk artists Katelyn and Laurie Shook.

[*Jay Blakesberg*]

115   **Contemplating an alter ego.**

"... Must I remain an unaggressive NP type for the rest of my life? ... Why can't I — by sheer will power — change my personality?!"

Many individuals have wondered if they could change their traits of personality simply by applying themselves to behave differently. Alas, any such effort is doomed to failure. Each one of us must live with our basic NPA personality type for our entire life... as if it were etched in stone.

[*Min An*]

PART 10

CHILDREN OF THE WORLD

116   **A sanguine family of N types.**

A sanguine infant begins to smile instinctively
during the first year of life.

[*Omar Medina, Dominican Republic*]

117   **A sanguine girl poses for holiday portrait.**

Even without a gingival smile, the presence of
the N trait is apparent.

[*Pixabay USA*]

118 **A non-sanguine girl poses for holiday portrait.**

In a non-sanguine individual, a neutral facial expression is the norm.

[*Ruslan Gilmanshin, Moscow*]

119   **Madonna with sanguine child.**

With the rosy cheeks and a coy demeanor, the trait of sanguinity in the child is apparent.

[*Pierre Mignard, ca. 1640, France*]

120   Madonna with non-sanguine child.

Here the facial complexion is more pallid and the demeanor more resolute.

Contrast the outstretched arms with the "narcissistic arms" pose of sanguinity (*see Plate 15*).

[*St. Isaac's Cathedral, ca. 1858, Russia*]

↓ **121**   **A non-sanguine boy with a calling to arms.**

Not having the N trait, non-sanguine A and PA
types have the fully expressed trait A of aggression.

[*Dariusz Sankowski, Poland*]

122   **Sanguine mother with non-sanguine child.**

If a sanguine mother has a non-sanguine child, NPA genetics dictate that the child's father must be non-sanguine, as well.

[*Chelsea Ferenando, Florida*]

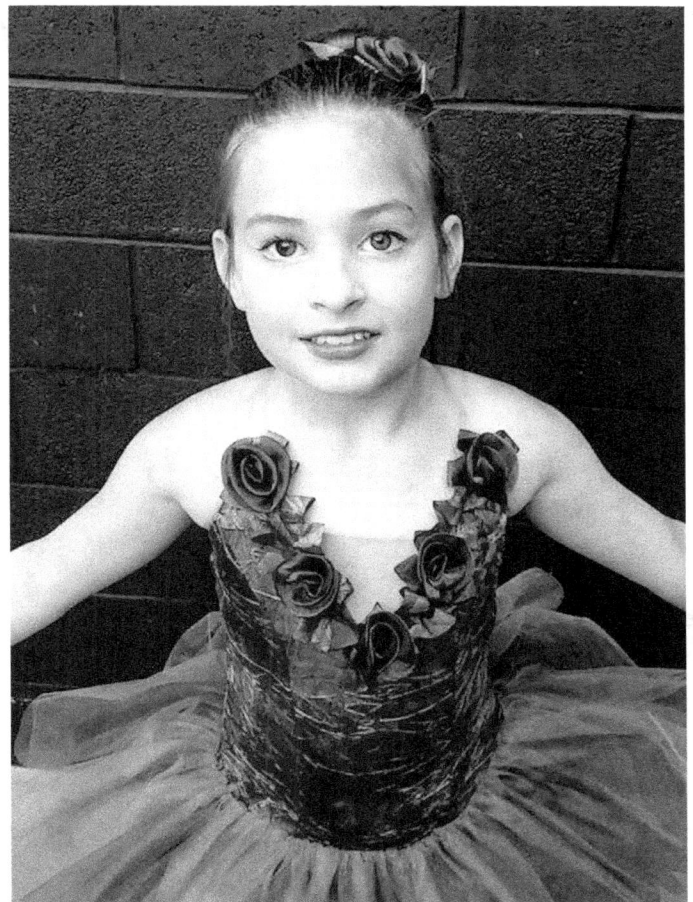

123   **A young sanguine ballerina.**

Among the performing arts, ballet is
especially attractive to sanguine types:
colorful costumes, expressive music,
and the possibility of recognition from
an appreciative audience.

[*Pam Simon, USA*]

←

124   **An NP boy tolerates his bossy sister.**

*"Instead of wasting time lining them up in
a row, why don't you just eat them?!"*

[*Alexis León, Chile*]

125   **Sanguine girl of the Mursi tribe, Ethiopia.**

Elaborate body adornment — beginning at an
early age — is part of everyday life in tribes of
the Omo Valley.

[*Rod Waddington*]

126   **Nomadic child of the Sudanese Desert.**

Embedded in a harsh environment, she manages
a trace of a smile of recognition during a fleeting
encounter with a passing visitor.

[*Christopher Michel*]

↓ 127   **NA boys swagger in Zambia.**

The boys wish to demonstrate to the visitor just how tough and aggressive they can be.

[*Alex Berger*]

↓ **128**   **Polite schoolboys in North Korea.**

With a smile of recognition, an NP boy, front and center, poses with his chums for a foreign visitor to their city.

[*Roman Harak*]

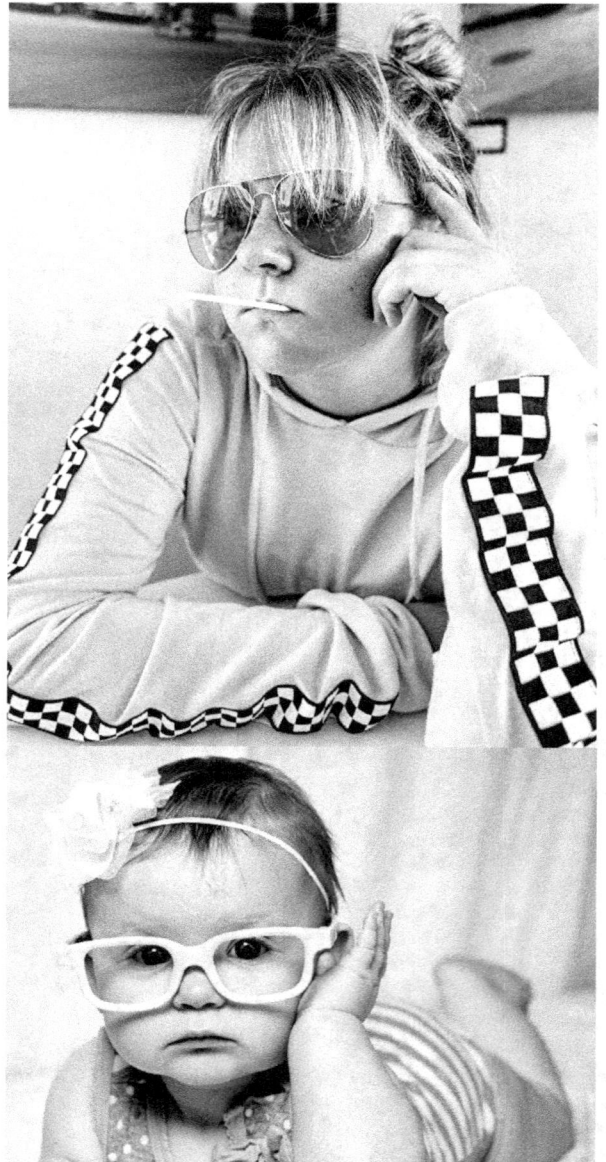

129   **Baby with yellow-frame eyeglasses and NA mom.**

NA mothers often dress their children in their own image, employing their favorite colors (yellow, pink, multi-colors). The woman above dressed in yellow, is not the baby's mother… but she just as well might be.

[*Dorothy Loges & Analise Benevides, USA*]

130   **Like father... like son.**

Very often a child is a "spitting image" of one of the parents (who may be very different)... a subtle reminder that one's basic personality type is transmitted in a packet of only a handful of genes.

[*Barry Lenard, USA*]

PART 11

ORIGINS AND GEOGRAPHY

131   **Evolutionary origins: the NPA traits in primates.**

As the NPA traits are genetically determined, they can be identified in other primates. Here, young male hamadryas baboons of northeast Africa pose for a portrait.

[*Brad*]

132   **Trait A: aggressive display in a baboon.**

A South African baboon displays his large canines.

Baboons are known for their intimidating aggressive behavior and strict "pecking order" societies based on dominance and submission.

[*Paolo Macorig*]

←

133   **Trait N: chest-thumping in a gorilla.**

In the sanguine, unaggressive gorilla, chest-thumping may be interpreted in terms of a "narcissistic display" of recognition. Rather than being aggressive, the gorilla is "showing off" his prowess.

[*Ryan Summers*]

134 **Trait P: perfectionistic use of tool in chimpanzee.**

Here, chimpanzees carefully "fish for termites" using sticks as a tool.

[*Margaret LaFarge*]

←

135 **Trait P: perfectionistic grooming in baboons.**

Here, a female hamadryas baboon carefully grooms a high-ranking male.

[*Dan Shouse*]

136   **Trait N: a "selfie" smile in an Old World monkey.**

An Indonesian macaque has the presence of mind to smile for a self-taken portrait.

[*Wikipedia*]

137 **Trait N: the chimpanzee smile.**

The sanguine smile is a good marker for the presence of the N trait in other primates. The smile is easily identified in all of the great apes, in many Old World monkeys… and perhaps in other species much more distant on the evolutionary time scale.

[*Valerie*]

↓ **138**   **Origins: the San Bushmen of southern Africa.**

Genetic evidence suggests that the San lineage is among the most ancient of any group of living peoples.

Very different from most other African tribes, the lighter-skinned San appear to be mostly sanguine, unaggressive NP types.

[*Fred Dawson*]

139   **Origins: the Australian Aborigines.**

Ancestors of the Aborigines are thought to be among the first groups to migrate "Out of Africa", some 65,000 years ago.

Present-day Aborigines consist mainly of two groups: the NA types of the central deserts and of Arnhem Land, and the NP types of the northern coast (*see Plate 157*).

The individual pictured is from Arnhem Land, and the non-perfectionistic use of body paint suggests that he is an NA type.

[*Rusty Stewart*]

↓ **140**   **East Africa: a Maasai tribesman.**

The unaggressive Maasai, known for their colorful adornment, gingival smiles and stylized vertical dancing, are identified as mainly N types.

[*A.J. Moore*]

↓ **141**   **West Africa: people of Nigeria.**

In contrast to northern East Africa, the A trait is prevalent in the west. In Nigeria, NA types predominate, as in this street scene from Abuja.

[*Mark Fischer*]

↓ **142**   **Mongolia: the "eagle girl".**

Present-day Mongolians are mostly N types.

It is easy to conjecture that the Mongol invasions of the Middle Ages were based on the trait of sanguinity, rather than on aggression.

[*David Baxendale*]

143   **Eastern Europe: Please do not smile for the camera.**

In Eastern Europe and Western Russia, non-sanguine A and PA types are common, and there is no tradition of requiring subjects to "smile for the camera".

Above, the locales are Latvia (*top*) and Belarus.

[*Rolands Lakis & Paval Hadzinski*]

↓ **144**   **Nomadic groups: Bedouin people.**

Nomadic groups, whether they be reindeer herders of the Arctic or the Romani "gypsies" of Europe, tend to be sanguine and non-perfectionistic. The Bedouins are Arab-speaking nomadic people, mainly in the Middle East. They appear to be mainly NA types.

[*Tribes of the World*]

↓ 145   Iran: a polymorphic region.

The people of Iran are a mixture of NPA types. Although non-sanguine types are definitely present, (*see Plate 36*), most of the population is sanguine, and the social smile is everywhere to be seen.

[*P. Liu*]

↓ **146**   **Indigenous America: people of the Peruvian Andes.**

With the colorful attire, the impression here is of sanguinity, and even the llama joins in the smiling.

From the Arctic regions to the Tierra del Fuego, indigenous America was sanguine and unaggressive, i.e., N and NP types.

[*Alexander Schimmeck*]

147   **Indigenous America: the Dakota People.**

The "Plains Indians" were renowned for their colorful attire and elaborate feathered headdresses. A mixture of N and NP types, the N types seem to have predominated.

[*Roderick Eime*]

148   **Polynesia: N types.**

Polynesia, with a paucity of both traits A and P, consists uniformly of N types. Thus, the intrepid sea voyagers who settled those Pacific Islands were likely mainly N types.

[*J. Utsler*]

149   **Maritime Southeast Asia: N types.**

Shown are women from the Philippines (*top*) and Sumatra. These are sanguine regions where the N type is the most prevalent.

[*Gezelle Rivera & Photobom*]

150   **Mainland southern Asia: N type in Thailand.**

N types are the most prevalent type in a broad expanse of southern Asia, including central India, Bangladesh, Thailand, Nepal, Tibet and much of southern China.

[*Sasin Tipchai*]

151   **Melanesia: NA types.**

In contrast to Polynesians, indigenous tribes in New Guinea, and the Melanesians to the east, have a high prevalence of A trait, being mainly NA types.

Above, women from Papua New Guinea.

[*David Kirkwood*]

152   **Modern America: the NA type of African heritage.**

Most African-Americans are descendants of slaves who were displaced to the New World from their homelands in West Africa (*see Plate 161*).

[*Jasmaine Cook & Efes Kitap*]

153 **Modern America: the NP farmer of the Midwest.**

The P trait was likely instrumental in the success of the agricultural revolution of the Neolithic Era in the Middle East and Europe.

The organized, industrious NP personality type seems ideal for a farmer.

[*Flickr*]

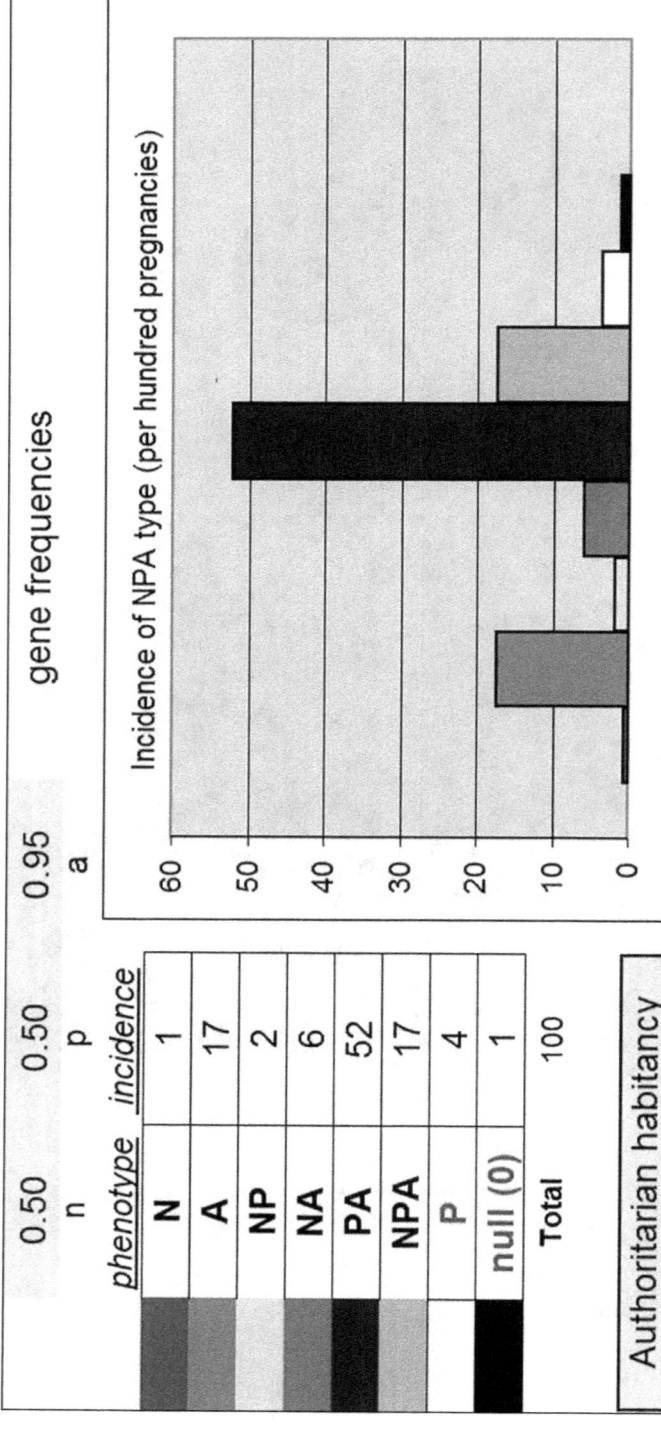

	0.50	0.50	0.95
	n	p	a

phenotype	incidence	
N	1	
A	17	
NP	2	
NA	6	
PA	52	
NPA	17	
P	4	
null (0)	1	
Total	100	

gene frequencies

Incidence of NPA type (per hundred pregnancies)

Authoritarian habitancy

154   **A non-sanguine population: the "Authoritarian habitancy".** On the basis of gene frequencies for the NPA traits, Hardy-Weinberg theory allows computation of the frequencies of NPA types in a population. Here. the PA type is the most common. followed by the A and NPA types.

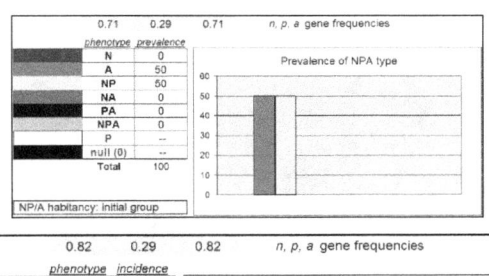

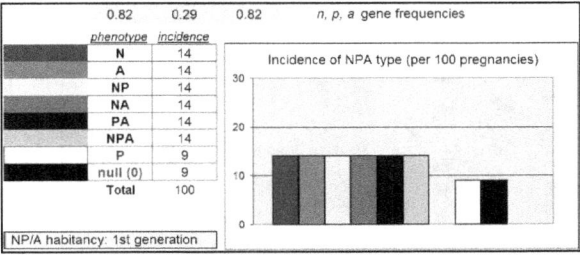

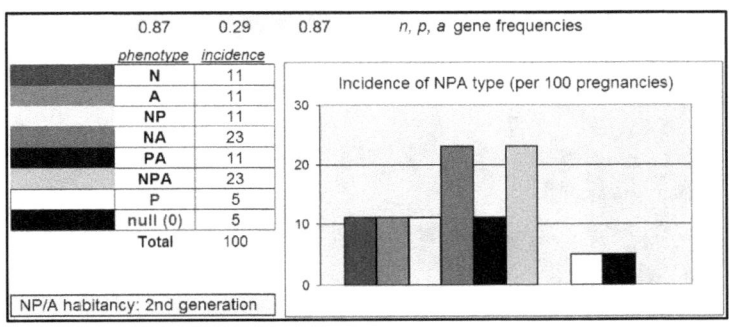

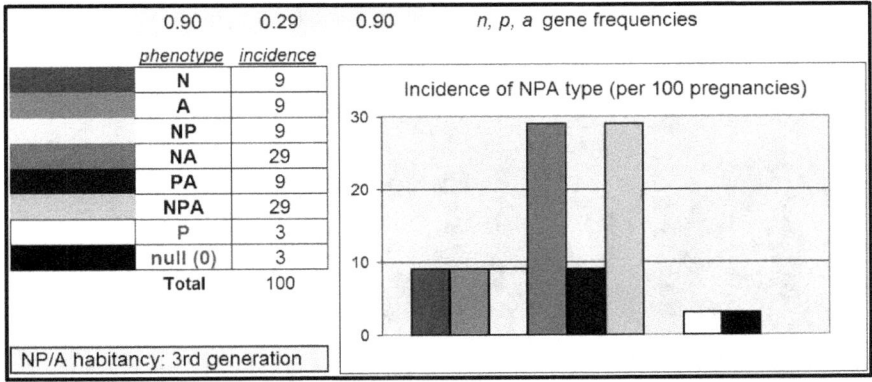

155 **NPA types in a population: successive generations.**

The graphs show types in three successive generations for a population initially composed equally of A and NP types. With each generation, the frequency of the "hybrid" NA and NPA types increases.

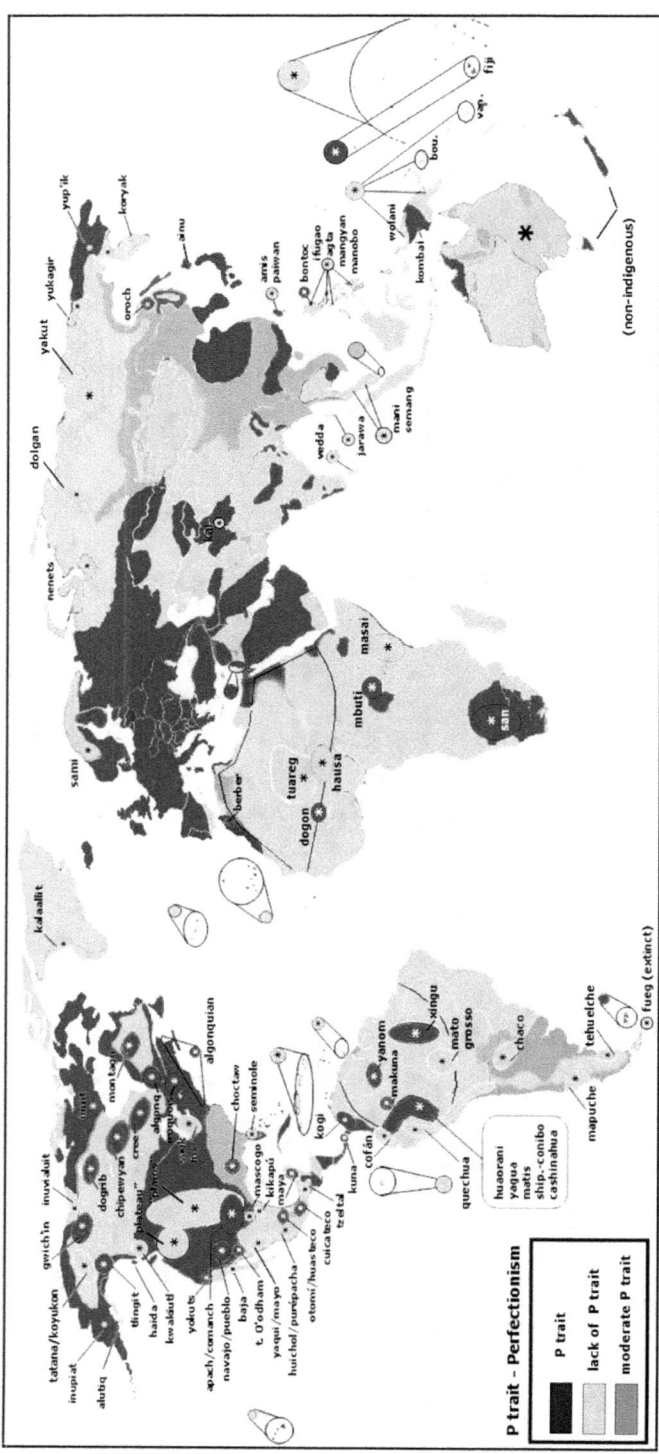

156   World map: distribution of the P trait. Notable is the paucity of P trait in most of Sub-Saharan Africa, Central Asia, Polynesia, and in the main group of Aborigines of Central Australia. The asterisks (*) denote indigenous peoples.

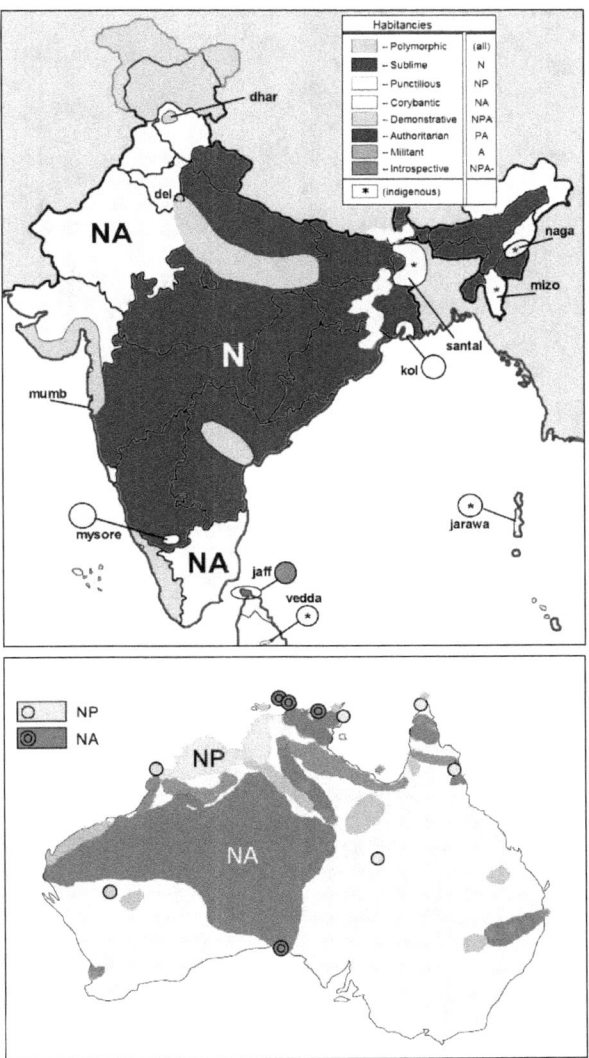

157 **Indian subcontinent and Aboriginal Australia.**

Top: India was found to be sanguine, with the dark
central region corresponding to a high prevalence
of N types, and the light regions in the northwest
and south indicating a majority of NA types.

Bottom: Present-day Aboriginal communities of
Australia. The main groups are 1) the NA types of
the central deserts and Arnhem Land, and 2) the
NP types of the northern coast.

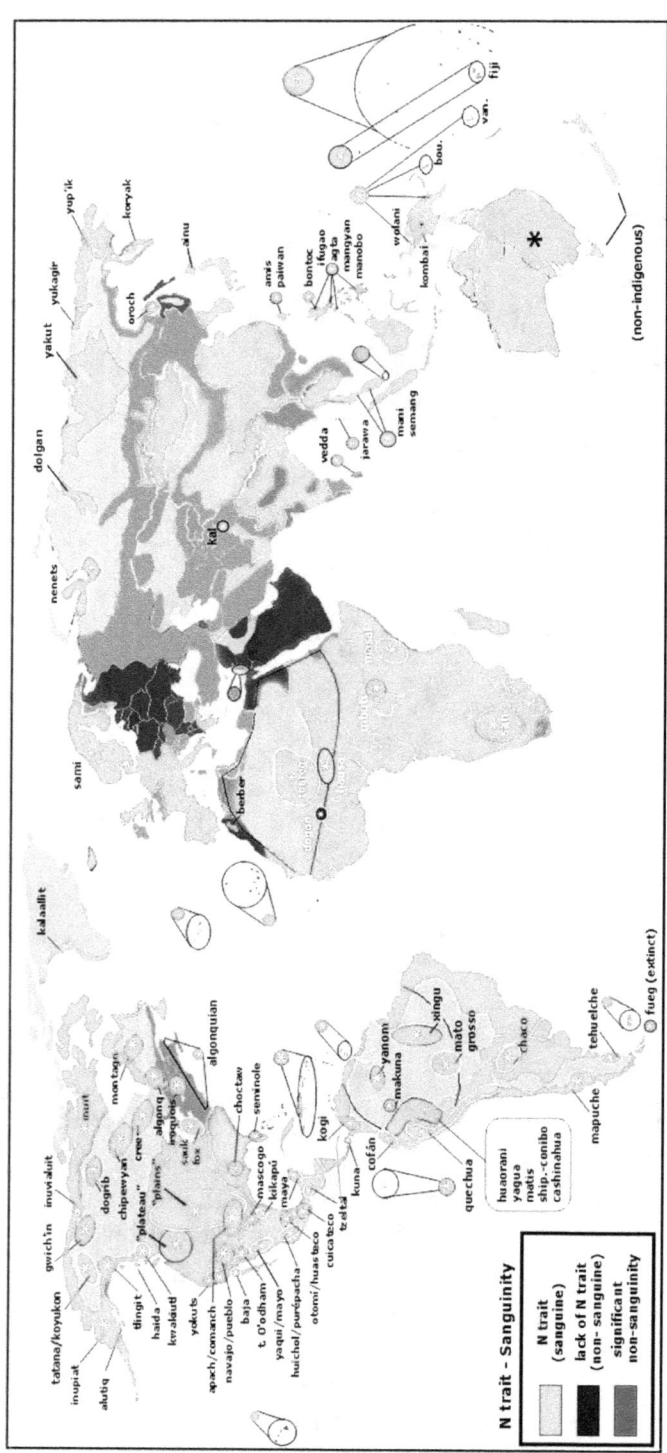

158   World map: distribution of non-sanguinity. Lack of the N trait is notable in the Middle East, Northern Africa, and Eastern Europe.

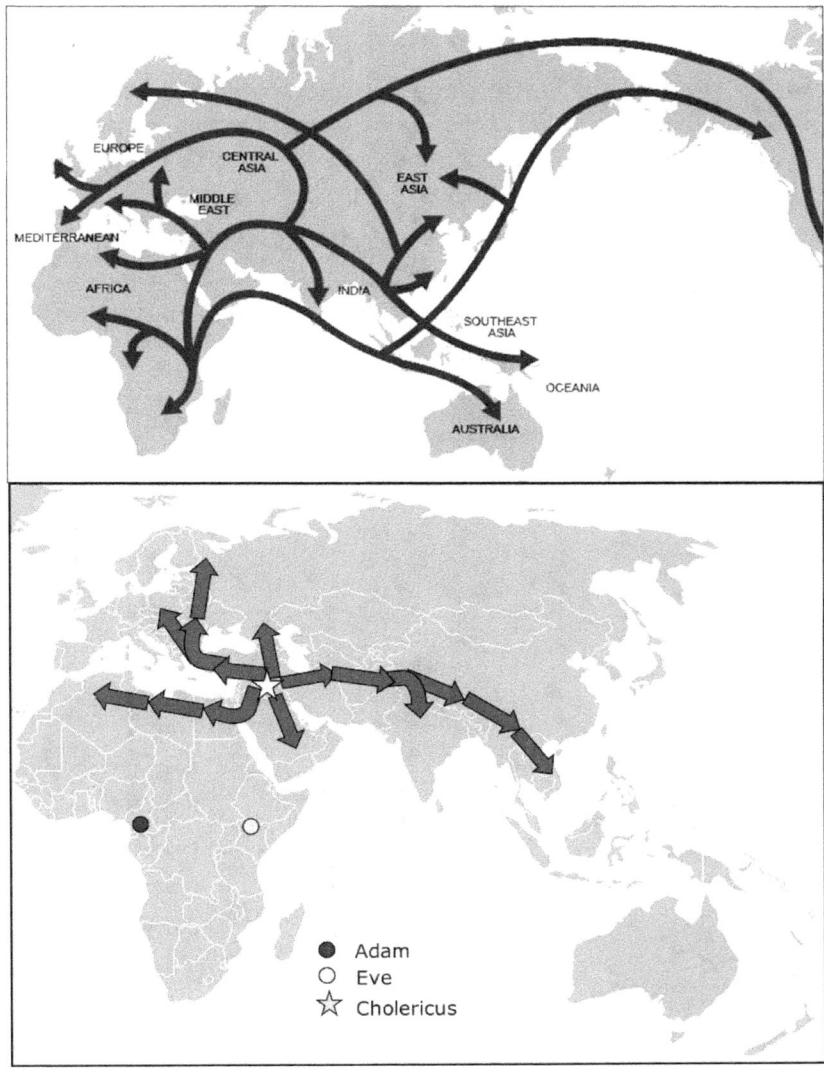

159   **"Out of Africa" and the origin of non-sanguinity.**

Top: Routes of ancestral migrations of *Homo sapiens*, as determined in studies of m-DNA and Y-chromosomal markers by population geneticists. [*Genographic Project*]

Bottom: Proposed non-sanguine geographic trails (lack of N trait) emanating from a founding individual, *Cholericus*, consistent with the "Out of Africa" ancestral migrations. The presumed locations of ancestral Y-chromosomal "Adam" and m-DNA "Eve" are also shown.

↓ 160   Territoriality and warfare: the Aztec example.

Inter-tribal hostility and fierce territorial behavior was found to be the norm in all types of indigenous peoples, hence it was not confined to those groups having a high prevalence of the A trait of aggression.

Below, a page from an Aztec pictorial manuscript, *ca.* 1535. The highly perfectionistic Aztec people were likely to have been mainly NP types.

[*Bodelian Library*]

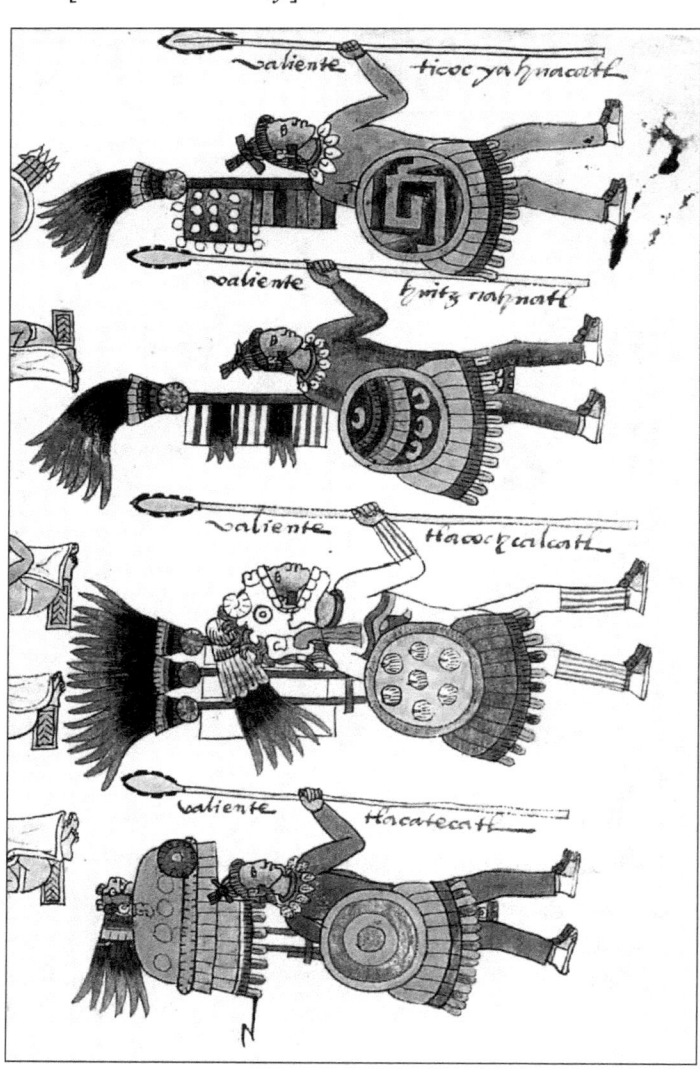

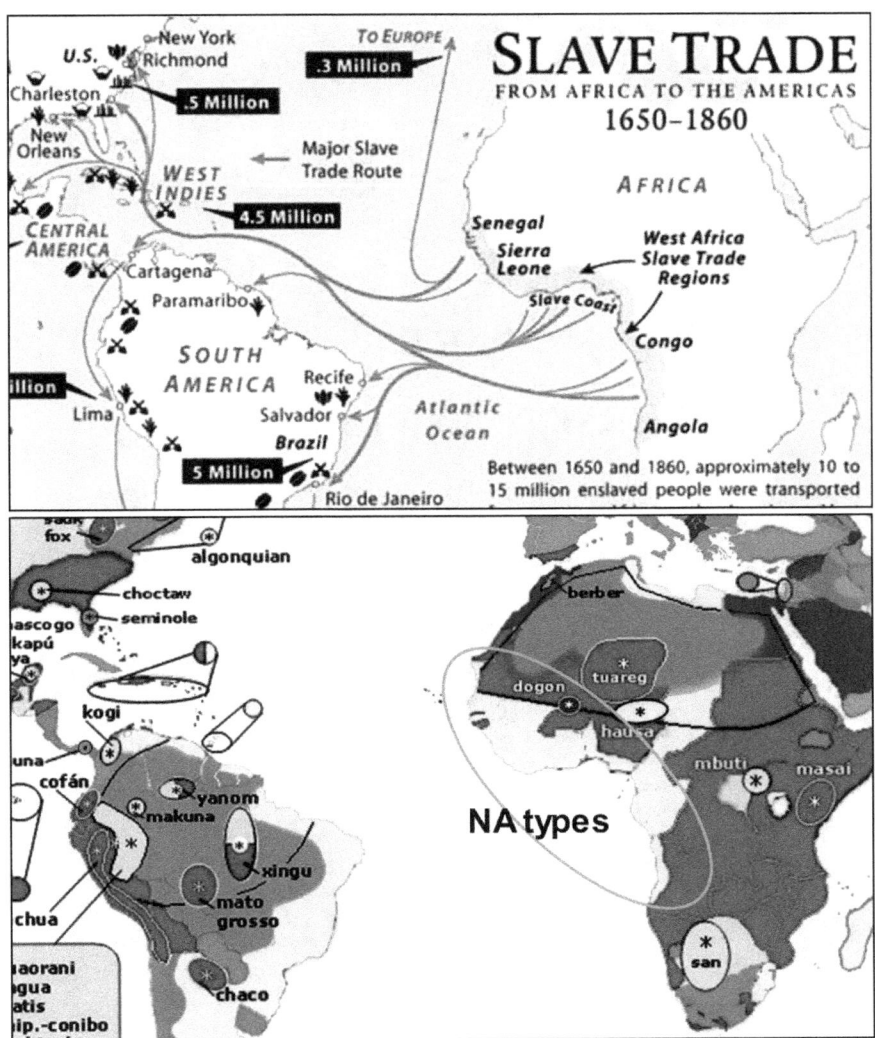

161   **Slave trade from West Africa: a region of high NA prevalence.**

Top: Primary routes of the slave trade.

Bottom: Map showing a predominance of NA types (light area) in the region from Senegal to Angola. This "Habitancy map" was produced from archival sources by estimating the most prevalent NPA types, country by country, in present-day Africa.

PART 12

DIVERSITY AND DISABILITY

162 **Diversity: intimate relationships.**

Whether the partners in a liaison are of the same or opposite sex, the dynamics of the relationship are governed mainly by the NPA types of the individuals.

[*Anastasiya Gepp*]

163   Obsessive-compulsive personality disorder.

The NP type is the one that is most likely to acquire the diagnosis of obsessive-compulsive personality disorder, or OCPD.

[*Nathan Penlington*]

164   The autistic savant: a perfectionist.

Autistic savants, as well as most individuals in the autistic spectrum, appear to be highly perfectionistic, unaggressive NP types.

Above, Daniel Tammet can recite from memory, in just a few hours, the irrational number Pi to over 20,000 decimal places.

[*Wikipedia*]

165   Antisocial personality disorder.

One subset of individuals having sociopathic tendency
is that of non-sanguine, non-perfectionistic A types.

[*Clem Onojeghuo*]

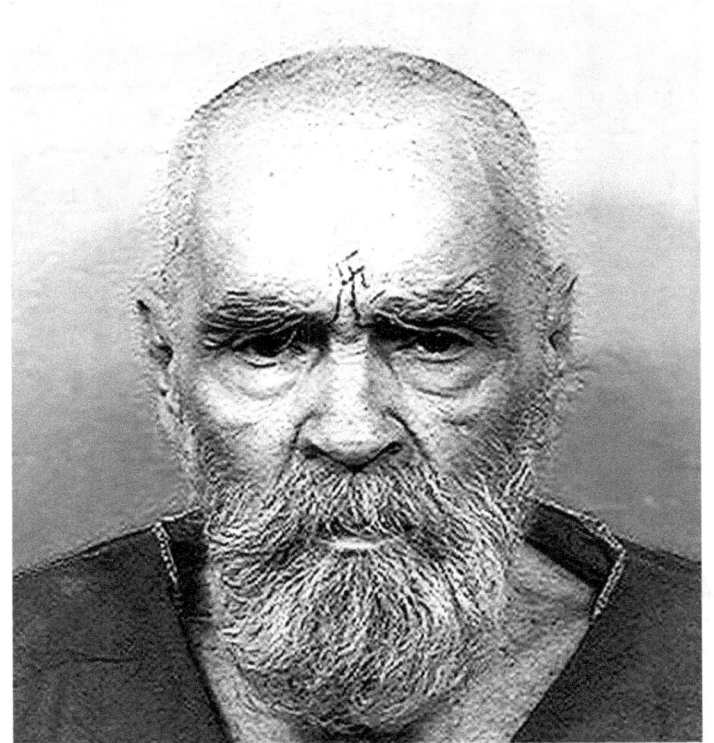

166 **Sadistic personality disorder: the A trait gone astray.**

Classic sadism is rooted in the A trait of the NPA model.

Above, an infamous A type: Charles Manson in 2017.

[*California Department of Corrections*]

167   Narcissistic personality disorder: the N trait gone astray.

"... Mirror, mirror, on the wall. Who is fairest of them all?"

The most likely personality types to acquire the diagnosis of "NPD" are the NA type, as depicted above, and the N type.

Just as sadism is rooted in the A trait, NPD has its basis in the N trait of the NPA model.

[Alessandro Baffa]

168 **Bipolar or manic-depressive disorder.**

In bipolar disorder, the individual may alternate between periods of elevated mood and depression.

Most individuals who acquire this diagnosis are sanguine and lack the P trait, i.e., they tend to be N, NA, NA− and NA= types.

[*Gerd Altmann*]

169   **Down's syndrome: an unaggressive child.**

Most children with Down's syndrome
appear to be unaggressive N or NP types.

Do older N or NP type mothers have a
higher propensity to have a child with
Down's syndrome?

[*Wikipedia*]

170   **Panic disorder: a genetic predisposition.**

Panic attacks often occur in social situations, for
example in an individual having the A− trait who is
suddenly called upon to speak in public. But they can
also occur in situations where the triggering cause is
obscure, as pictured at left.

[*Flavio Spugna*]

171   **Introversion: a genetic predisposition.**

Many introverted individuals have the A−
trait of inhibited aggression, sometimes to the
extent of having a "social phobia".

Above, actor Anthony Perkins plays the role
of an introverted loner who descends into
psychopathology in Hitchcock's film,
"Psycho".

[*Flickr*]

←

172   **Explosive rages: a genetic predisposition.**

Uncontrollable rages most often occur in
individuals having the A trait, and especially in
volatile NA types.

Most often, the object of the rage is another
individual, but sometimes it is an inanimate object,
as pictured at left.

[*Reid Rosenberg*]

173   Attention deficit hyperactivity disorder.

The NA type is especially vulnerable to ADHD and other disorders of impulse control. With its genetic predisposition, signs of hyperactivity appear at an early age.

[*Richard Yu*]

174   **Post traumatic stress disorder.**

Also genetically predisposed, the PTS syndrome occurs especially in vulnerable individuals having the A− trait.

Above, a soldier wounded on Hill 1171 during the Korean conflict, 1951.

[*U.S. Army*]

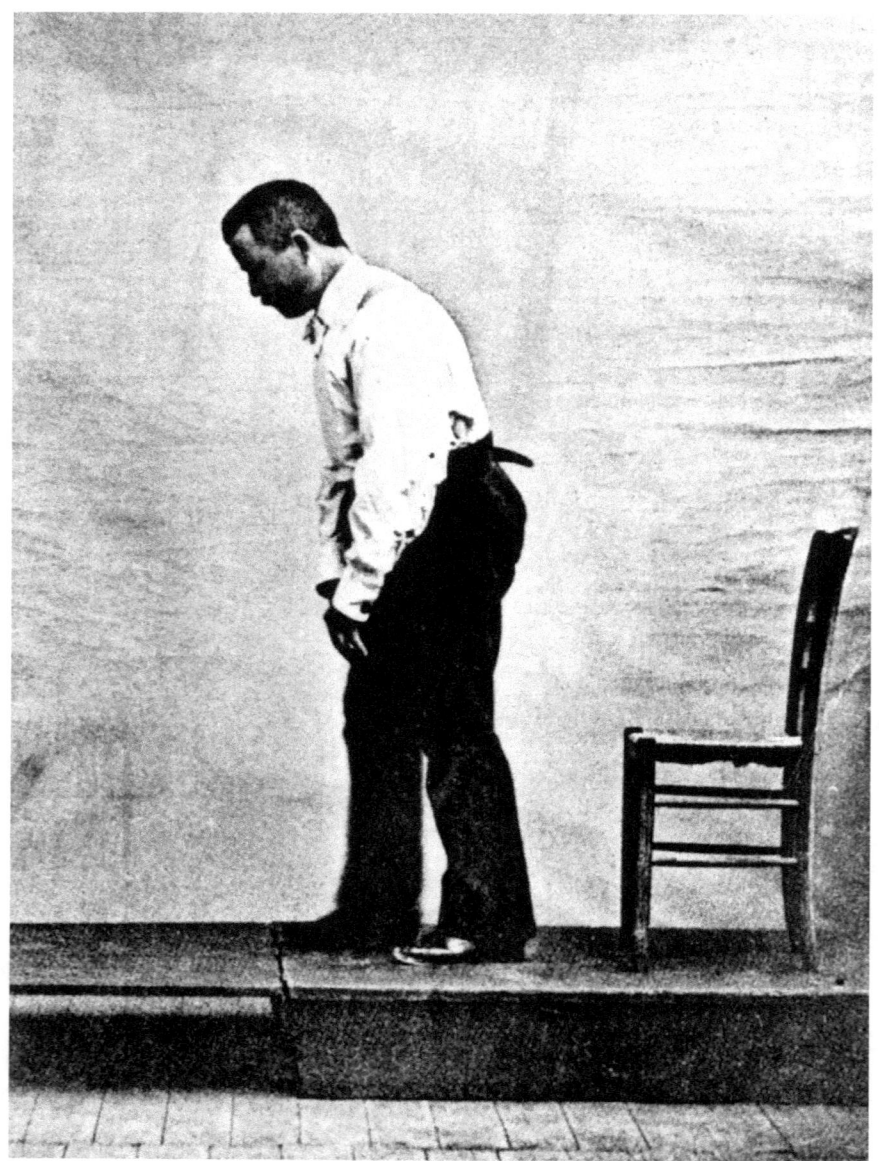

175   Parkinson's disease: a condition linked to A− trait.

Individuals with "Parkinson's" typically have the A− trait of inhibited aggression from childhood.

Signs of the disease include muscular rigidity, postural instability and a coarse hand tremor.

[*La Salpêtrière*]

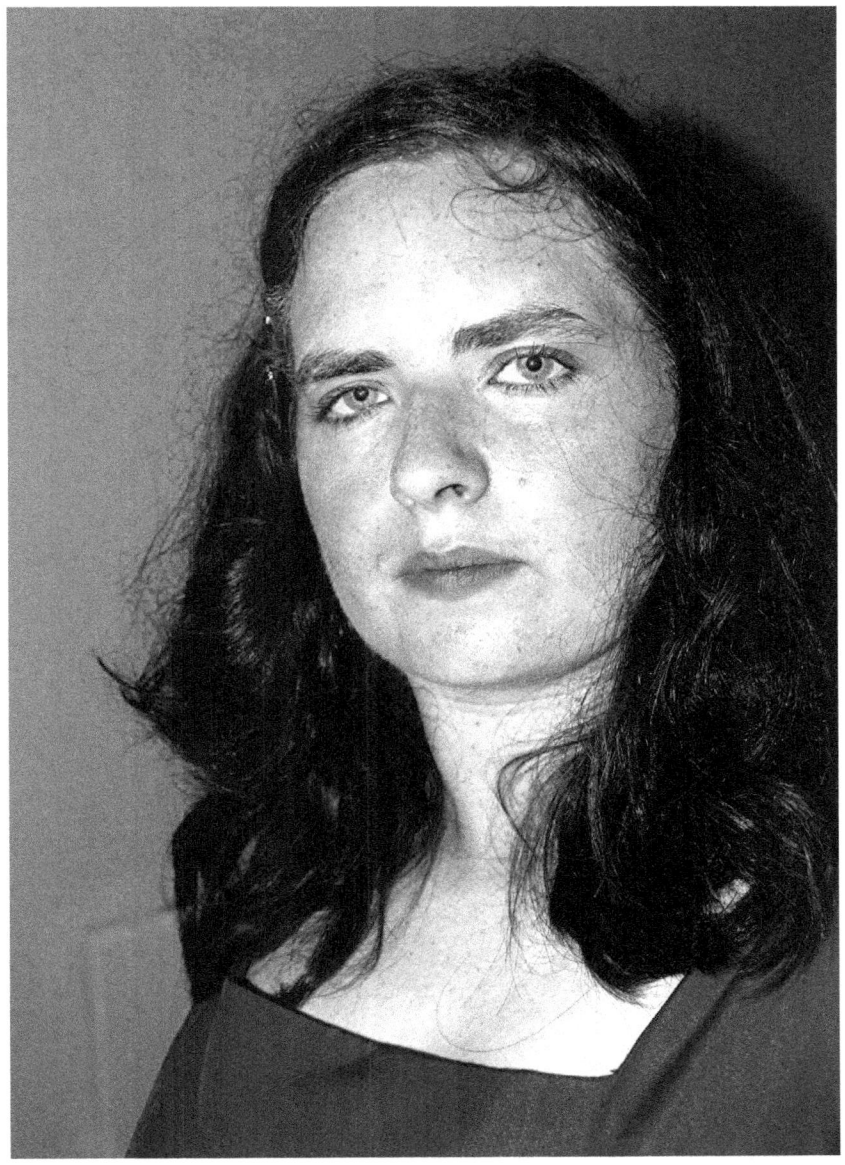

176 **Eczema: a skin condition linked to A− trait.**

Individuals with "atopic dermatitis" often have the A− trait, as illustrated in the NPA− type.

According to NPA genetics, N or NP types with eczema (who lack the A trait) can be silent carriers of the A− trait.

[*Sarahluv UK*]

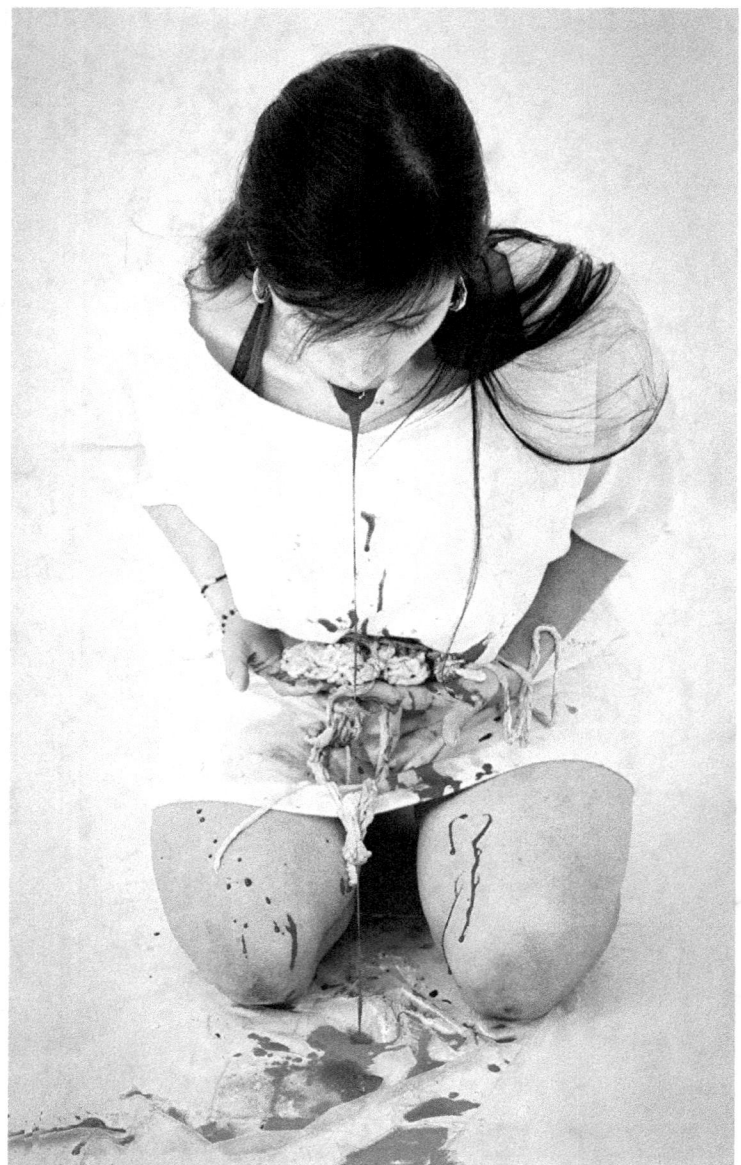

177   Bulimia: an eating disorder related to lack of P trait.

In Western society, most individuals with bulimia are sanguine, non-perfectionistic N, NA and NA− types. However, in other eating disorders, such as anorexia nervosa, perfectionism may be a risk factor.

[*Julián Gaitán*]

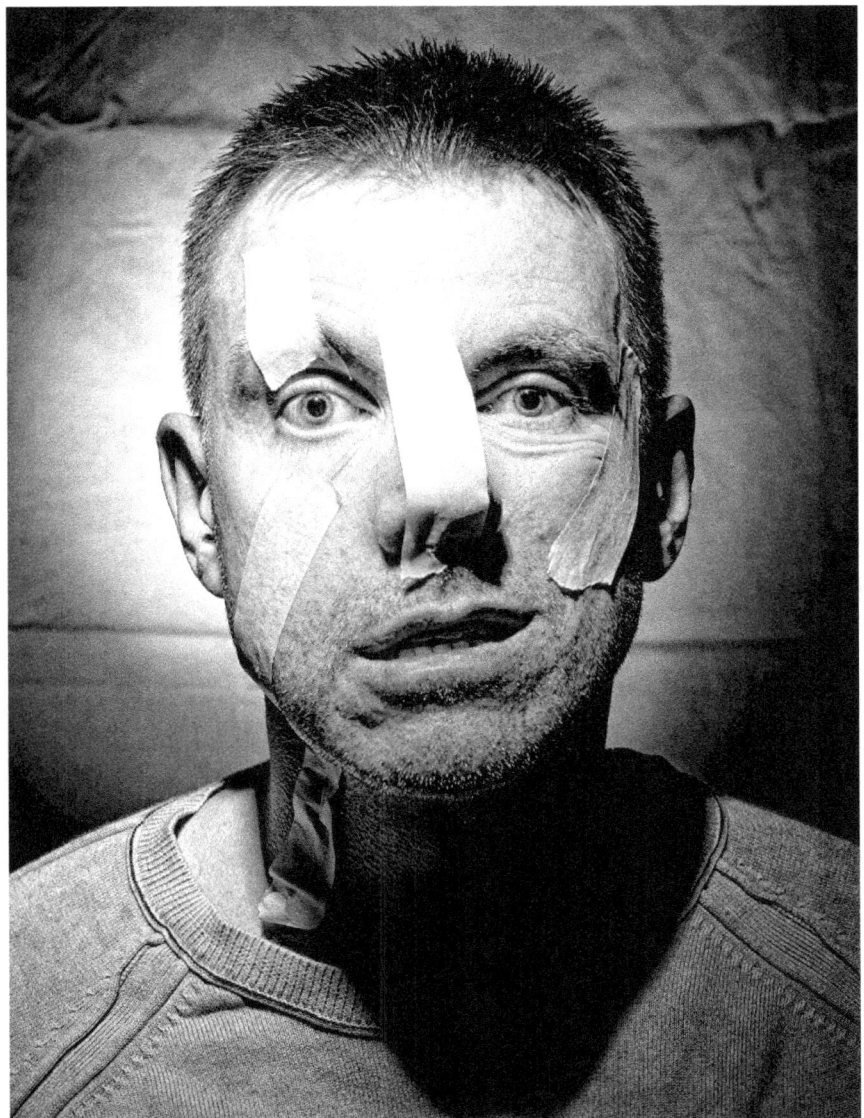

178   **Borderline NPA personality types.**

Borderline types in the NPA model are those in whom neither trait N nor trait A is fully expressed.

Future generations will need to face the issue that in some parental matches, fragile Borderline types will appear predictably among the children.

[*David Blackwell*]

↓ **179**   **Schizophrenia: social isolation.**

Schizophrenia is highly multifactorial, but the NPA
model suggests that some character types have a higher
genetic predisposition to the condition.

[Dmitry Sladkov]

APPENDIX

APPENDIX

NPA PERSONALITY THEORY: SYNOPSIS

Personality theory based on the genetic traits of sanguinity, perfectionism and aggression

Contents

- 1 What is personality?
- 2 NPA model based on three genetic traits
  - 2.1 Genetics and environment
  - 2.2 Traits of sanguinity, perfectionism and aggression
    - 2.2.1 Aggression (A)
    - 2.2.2 Sanguinity (N)
    - 2.2.3 Perfectionism (P)
- 3 Character types
  - 3.1 Dominance: dominant types
    - 3.1.1 N type
    - 3.1.2 A type
    - 3.1.3 NA type
    - 3.1.4 NP type
    - 3.1.5 PA type
    - 3.1.6 NPA type
  - 3.2 Submission: Passive Aggressive types
    - 3.2.1 Non-compliant types
    - 3.2.2 Compliant types
  - 3.3 Resignation: Resigned types
- 4 Borderline types and mental illness
- 5 Dominance and submission
- 6 Mendelian transmission of NPA traits
- 7 Implications of a trait theory based on genetics
  - 7.1 Population Genetics
  - 7.2 Evolutionary origins of NPA traits
  - 7.3 Predictive aspects of NPA model
- 8 Criticism and controversy
- 9 References
- 10 Citations
- 11 Illustrations
- 12 Source

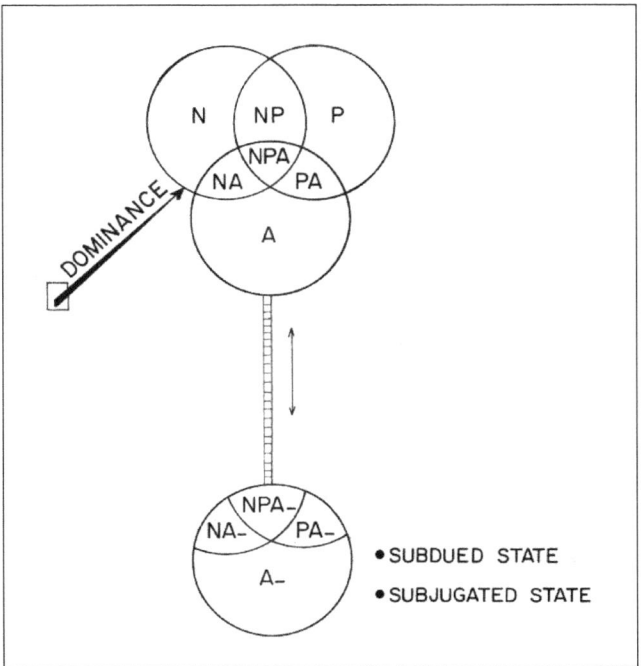

Fig. A1. Venn diagram of Dominant character types. Character types having the trait of aggression A may be reduced, reversibly, to a subdued or subjugated state A–.

The NPA theory of personality was developed by A.M. Benis on the basis of concepts presented over fifty years ago by psychiatrist Karen Horney. The model posits three major behavioral traits underlying personality: sanguinity (N), perfectionism (P) and aggression (A), leading to the formulation of discrete character types. Each trait is based on a major pleiotropic gene (a gene determining several related characteristics) that follows the rules of Mendelian genetics.

The NPA model proposes that the character traits A and N are indispensable to human development, being related to the sympathetic and parasympathetic nervous systems, respectively. The trait P is also assumed to function at the level of the central nervous system and to act as a modifier of the expression of traits A and N. The NPA model proposes to clarify the genetic bases of known personality disorders, diseases related to behavioral factors ("psychosomatic diseases") and mental illnesses. An online NPA personality test is available in English and other language versions.

What is personality?

Psychologists speak of personality as "a collection of emotional, thought and behavioral patterns unique to a person that is consistent over time" [1]. Although many investigators have proposed various theories of personality, no objectively testable model has emerged. The NPA model falls into the category of a trait theory of personality, its unique approach being that it is biologically based on classical human genetics.

NPA model based on three genetic traits

Genetics and environment

Although it is universally accepted that both genetic and environmental factors (or "nature and nurture") comprise personality, the relevant genes have yet to be identified [2]. Studies of the heritability of personality factors conducted with identical and fraternal twins emphasize the importance of genetics in behavior [3]. The NPA model acknowledges the possible importance of environment and culture in personality but emphasizes that it is the genetic, or structural, factors that first need to be identified.

The NPA model acknowledges that the genetic bases of personality are themselves complex. It assumes at least four tiers to this genetic basis:

- male or female gender
- character type based on the three NPA traits
- temperament, or the degree of activity or excitability of an individual in the Pavlovian sense
- other facets of personality, such as Raymond Cattell's 16 Personality Factors or Hans Eysenck's P-E-N model of personality.

The NPA model, thus, focuses on only the second of these four tiers, acknowledging that temperament and other facets of personality may involve a large number of genes.

Traits of sanguinity, perfectionism and aggression

Karen Horney (Fig. A2) advanced the concept that at maturity there exist at least three expansive character types, namely the "narcissistic", the "perfectionistic" and the "arrogant-vindictive" [5].

Fig. A2. Karen Horney (1885-1952)

Extending these ideas, the NPA model posits that the human character rests primarily on the existence of three major traits: sanguinity (N), perfectionism (P) and aggression (A). Each of these traits is assumed to exist as the expression of a single major pleiotropic gene. Horney considered that the traits have environmental origins, being the result of an individual's desperate search for dominance in the context of a stifling upbringing [5]. The NPA model — in ascribing the traits to genetic origins — emphasizes biological attributes associated with the traits.

Aggression (A)

The behavioral trait of aggression is proposed to be the most labile of the three [6]. The stereotypic acts associated with this trait involve body posturing, gestures, and eye contact of intimidation and deference, with individuals having this trait continually competing with each other on a scale of dominance and submission. The trait of aggression corresponds to a striving for *power* over one's environment, hence it is one main component of competitiveness in social relations, or ambition. In a pejorative connotation the trait may reveal itself in the context of sadism or sadomasochism. The facial expression is non-sanguine, i.e., tending toward sallowness or pallor in individuals of light skin color. The hallmark of the trait of aggression is a mass discharge of the sympathetic nervous system: the "flight or fight" response or the aggressive-vindictive rage. During the expression of this rage, the facial complexion of pallor is accentuated.

Sanguinity (N)

The trait of sanguinity (Horney's "narcissism") is proposed to be less labile than that of aggression (where individuals may be constantly altering their character states on a scale of dominance and submission) [6]. The stereotypic acts associated with the trait include self-flaunting body posturing, expansive arm gestures, bowing, instinctive self-adornment, and a natural attraction to the limelight of personal recognition. Individuals having only this trait (of the three) are competitive but non-aggressive in their strivings for recognition. The trait corresponds to a striving for *glory* in one's environment, representing the second main component of human ambition. In the absence of mediating factors, the unbridled trait of sanguinity may reveal itself in the context of conceit, exhibitionism, vanity or messianism. An associated facial expression includes the radiant gingival smile (broadly exposing the gums and teeth). The facial complexion in individuals of light skin color tends toward blood-red or ruddy. Hallmarks of the trait include blushing, flushing, and a mass discharge of the autonomic nervous system: the narcissistic rage of defense and withdrawal. During expression of this rage the normally sanguine complexion becomes even more florid.

Perfectionism (P)

The trait of perfectionism in the NPA model is not a basic drive of ambition and is not associated with a rage reaction [6]. Rather it is a mediator of the unbridled drives of aggression and/or sanguinity. The stereotypic acts associated with the trait of perfectionism are obsessiveness, compulsiveness, repetition, and the maintenance of neatness, order and symmetry. A clue to the nature of the trait lies in the compulsive, repetitive mannerisms of autistic children and some adult schizophrenic individuals. The behavioral pattern is often ritualistic and the speech characterized by echolalia. It is posited that such autistic and schizophrenic individuals are those in whom the two components of ambition, i.e., aggression and sanguinity, have been suppressed by genetic or environmental factors, either congenitally, in childhood, or after maturity, thus revealing in the individual a primitive state of perfectionism.

Fig. A3. Character types according to the ancient theory of humors: *Phlegmaticus, Cholericus, Sanguineus* and *Melancholicus.* [*J.K. Lavater, ca. 1775*]

Character types

The notion that humans exhibit only a limited number of discrete character types can be traced back to the time of the ancient Greeks, in particular to the theory of humors (blood, black bile, yellow bile and phlegm): see Fig. A3. The NPA model attempts to relate genetic NPA types to these character types of antiquity, as well as to the classic personality disorders of modern psychiatry.

Dominance: Dominant character types

In Dominant types the traits A and N, if present at all, are fully expressed [6]. The NPA model generates the following dominant character types:

N type

The *sanguine (N) type* is found in the writings of Horney [7] and others who have developed the classic psychiatric views of narcissism. In the NPA model, this type is the equivalent of the sanguine character type described by the ancients. The important attributes of this type are: expansiveness but unaggressiveness, non-perfectionism, a tendency to flamboyant self-adornment, a natural attraction to the limelight, the gingival smile of recognition and the florid narcissistic rage. In extreme forms this type appears as a self-anointed visionary, a proselytizing evangelist or a messianic personality.

A type

The *aggressive (A) type* corresponds to Horney's arrogant-vindictive type and to her concept of "moving against people" [8]. In the NPA model this is the classic choleric character type of antiquity. The main attributes of this type are: unbridled arrogance, instinctual vindictiveness, non-perfectionism, no tendency to self-adornment, a wry or sardonic grin in place of a gingival smile, and the pallid-complexioned aggressive-vindictive rage. In extreme forms this type appears as a sadistic personality, as an extroverted paranoid personality, or as the so-called antisocial or sociopathic personality.

NA type

The *sanguine-aggressive (NA) type* is regarded to be a composite of the previously described sanguine and aggressive types. Horney described the essence of this character type, in the female, in an article, "The overvaluation of love: a study of a common present day type" [9]. The main attributes of this type are: a sanguine complexion, synergistic merging of unbridled narcissism and aggression, hyperactivity, non-perfectionism, a tendency toward extreme self-adornment, exhibitionism in the limelight, a "flashy" extroverted smile and a tendency toward aggressive-vindictive or combined narcissistic-aggressive rages. In extreme forms this type appears as the hypomanic, histrionic or hysterical personality.

NP type

The attributes of the *sanguine-perfectionist (NP) type* were described by Horney in her exposition of the "perfectionist type" [4]. In the NPA model this encompasses the classic phlegmatic type known to the ancients. The main qualities of this type are: a tendency toward a sanguine complexion, industriousness, orderliness, an intense sense of duty, unaggressiveness, stubbornness, negativism, a tendency to ruminate, perfectionistic rather than unbridled self-adornment, an uncommonly seen gingival smile of recognition, and the capacity to exhibit the florid narcissistic rage. In extreme forms this character appears as the obsessive-compulsive personality.

PA type

The *perfectionistic-aggressive (PA)* type is alluded to by Horney in her mention of aggressive types who function in the capacity of a "power behind the throne" [8], that is, personages who utilize intellectual qualities and planning rather than overt aggression to achieve their aims. In the NPA model this is the classic non-sanguine, austere melancholic personality of the ancients. The principal qualities of this type are: a non-sanguine complexion, passive-aggressive behavior, dour perfectionism, vigilance, manipulativeness, a proud bearing, haughty reservedness, a calculated vindictiveness, a lack of an innate tendency to self-adornment, a sardonic grin, and the pallid aggressive-vindictive rage. In extreme forms this is the passive-aggressive, rebellious-distrustful, or ruminating paranoid personality.

NPA type

The *sanguine-perfectionistic-aggressive (NPA) type* was not explicitly described by Horney, although she did note that the three traits can coexist in the same individual [10]. The main attributes of this type are: a sanguine complexion, a loud voice, dynamism with a tendency to be overbearing, bombastic garrulity, intense eye contact, a strong sense of duty, a bent toward conventional values, unpretentious self-adornment, an outgoing smile of moderate intensity, and the capacity to exhibit the narcissistic, aggressive, or explosive narcissistic-aggressive rages. In the extreme cases, this individual is the managerial-autocratic or explosive personality.

Submission: Passive Aggressive character types

In Passive Aggressive types the trait of aggression is not fully expressed [6]. The NPA model defines two gradations of relative submission: *non-compliance*, in which the individual is basically submissive but is easily activated to an energetic state of aggression, and *compliance*, in which the individual tends to remain in a profound state of submission.

In the model the state of submission, or inhibition of aggression, most often has a genetic basis, the result of a congenital, incomplete expression of the gene for the trait A. However, the model also allows for environmental causes, the state of submission being induced during the juvenile period on the basis of environmental constraints to character development. That is, phenocopies (based on environmental factors) of a genetically disposed submissive state may exist. Also, like

Dominant types having full expression of the trait A, Passive Aggressive types may exhibit the aggressive A rage.

Non-compliant types

The model denotes the state of non-compliance by A–, obtaining the following *non-compliant* phenotypes:

- **Aggressive (A–)**
- **Perfectionistic-aggressive (PA–)**
- **Sanguine (NA–)**
- **Sanguine-perfectionistic (NPA–)**

Compliant types

The model denotes the state of compliance by A=, obtaining the following *compliant* phenotypes:

- **Aggressive (A=)**
- **Perfectionistic-aggressive (PA=)**
- **Sanguine (NA=)**
- **Sanguine-perfectionistic (NPA=)**

The *NPA– non-compliant type* above corresponds to active, motivated, non-confrontational individuals whose baseline personality tends toward submissiveness, as described by Horney in her discussion of "inverted sadistic" behavior [11]. In the therapeutic setting, these individuals are found over the spectrum of the "Type A", dependent, and phobic-anxious personality. The *NA– type* is a non-perfectionistic, active individual, often exhibiting unbridled narcissistic behavior. In the therapeutic setting this is a cyclothymic or dependent histrionic personality.

The *compliant types NA=* and *NPA=* above correspond to more profoundly submissive individuals, having more pronounced tendencies toward masochistic behavior [12]. They correspond to Horney's compliant "self-effacing" personality and to her concept of "moving toward people" [13].

Resignation: Resigned character types

In the character state of resignation the trait of aggression is inhibited after maturity because of environmental constraints [6]. Unlike the Passive Aggressive types who readily involve themselves in the relative competition of dominance and submission (and sometimes sadomasochism), Resigned types remain relatively detached from such activities and only with difficulty can be stressed to an A+ state of active aggression. However, like Passive Aggressive types, the Resigned types can be induced into the aggressive A rage.

The model denotes the state of resignation by –A, obtaining the following resigned phenotypes:

- **Aggressive (–A)**
- **Perfectionistic-aggressive (P–A)**
- **Sanguine (N–A)**
- **Sanguine-perfectionistic (NP–A)**

The sanguine Resigned types, having the N trait, correspond to detached individuals, as described by Horney. She considered that "moving away from people" was a maladaptive response that could develop as a growing individual struggled toward maturity [14]. The *NP–A type* would tend to have strong perfectionistic tendencies, while the *N–A type* would be more labile.

Borderline types and mental illness

In the NPA model, *Borderline types* possess only one of the traits of ambition (N or A) and it is only partially expressed. Types in which both traits (N and A) are either absent or profoundly suppressed fall into categories of mental illness, in particular schizophrenia [6]. Thus, NPA model predicts that the categories of Borderline personality and schizophrenia are heterogeneous, depending on the underlying NPA character structure. Examples of Borderline types would be the A– or PA– types above. Types falling into the categories of mental illness would be the compliant Passive Aggressive types, A= or PA=.

One aspect of the model focuses on the Dominant types N and NP, which lack the trait A [6]. In analogy with partial expression of the trait A, the theory identifies states of incomplete expression of the trait N, denoted as N–, N= and –N. Examples of such Borderline types would be N– or N– P types. Types falling into the categories of mental illness would be N= or N=P, the latter being a perfectionistic, autistic individual.

Dominance and submission

In the NPA model, Dominant character types having the trait A have the potential of being reduced to an A– subdued state acutely or to a subjugated state chronically (see Fig. A1 above). Similarly, non-compliant Passive Aggressive types have the potential of being activated to an energetic A+ state resembling dominance, usually for short periods of time. Thus, the model emphasizes the potential lability of trait A in social relations, with Dominant and Passive Aggressive types continually altering their behavior in competitive interactions with other individuals and in the context of mating. In the extreme, some of these relationships fall into the category of sadomasochism [15]. Resigned types, in their detachment from social interactions, steadfastly avoid dominance-submission relationships and, in particular, hierarchal structures where "pecking orders" predominate.

Mendelian transmission of NPA traits

On the basis of archetypal examples, the model assumes that in their full expression the NPA traits are transmitted by autosomal genes, with traits A and N being recessive and trait P being transmitted in the dominant mode [6]. The alleles corresponding to full expression and total suppression of the trait A are denoted by a and A_0, respectively, and the corresponding alleles for the trait N are denoted by n and N_0. For the trait P two alleles P and p_0 are posited, corresponding to full expression or total absence of the trait P, on the assumption that the trait is transmitted with complete penetrance. This scheme of inheritance is consistent with the notion that the alleles A_0 and N_0 control the production of inhibitors of the traits A and N at the level of the central nervous system, with alleles A_0 and N_0 being dominant with respect to a and n. The scheme leads directly to Table A1, showing the possible phenotypes of progeny according to the phenotypes of the parents:

Table A1 shows:

- N and A individuals need not have N or A parents. Such individuals can arise *de novo* so long as at least one of the parents is an NP and PA individual, respectively.

- PA individuals must have at least one parent who is of either the PA or A type.

- NP individuals must have at least one parent who is of either the NP or N type.

- NA individuals can arise *de novo* from any combination of phenotypes.

	N	A	NP	NA	PA	NPA
N	N -- -- NA -- -- -- -- --	"	"	"	"	"
A	N -- -- NA -- -- 0 A	-- -- -- NA -- -- -- A	"	"	"	"
NP	N NP -- NA NPA -- -- --	N NP P NA NPA PA 0 A	N NP -- NA NPA -- -- --	"	"	"
NA	N -- -- NA -- -- -- --	-- -- -- NA -- -- -- A	N NP -- NA NPA -- -- --	-- -- -- NA -- -- -- --	"	"
PA	N NP P NA NPA PA 0 A	-- -- -- NA NPA PA -- A	N NP P NA NPA PA 0 A	-- -- -- NA NPA PA -- A	-- -- -- NA NPA PA -- A	"
NPA	N NP -- NA NPA -- -- --	-- -- -- NA NPA PA -- A	N NP -- NA NPA -- -- --	-- -- -- NA NPA -- -- --	-- -- -- NA NPA PA -- A	-- -- -- NA NPA -- -- --
FATHER OR MOTHER	N	A	NP	NA	PA	NPA

Table A1. Possible phenotypes of children according to the phenotypes of the parents. The parental phenotypes are shown along the axes of the table. The P and null (0) phenotypes are non-viable and would result in miscarriage, stillbirth or an infant who fails to thrive.

- The mating of two NA types can yield progeny of only NA types.

- The mating of an NPA type with an NA type can yield progeny of only NPA or NA types.

- Certain combinations of parental genotypes may lead to zygotes having only the P trait (P phenotype) or lacking all three traits (null phenotype, denoted by 0). According to the NPA model, zygotes of P or null phenotype would be non-viable. Thus, the model predicts *partial* or *complete infertility* in a limited number of combinations of parental phenotypes, these being N×A, N×PA, NP×A and NP×PA.

Implications of a trait theory based on genetics

Population Genetics

A trait theory based on genetics would imply that the personality structure of a population could be expressed in definitive mathematical terms. The NPA model is amenable to the Hardy-Weinberg approach to quantify the distribution of NPA character types in a given subpopulation [16]. With the usual assumptions of gene frequencies n, p and a and random mating, incidences of Dominant character types are given in Table A2 below. Because of the occurrence of non-viable P and null (0) phenotypes, the assumptions of Hardy-Weinberg equilibrium would not be strictly valid: the incidences generated by the expressions in Table A2 represent the phenotypes of the first generation only.

The assumption of numerical values for the three gene frequencies n, p and a generates a hypothetical subpopulation, or "habitancy" [16]. In Table A3 below, six habitancies are presented with descriptive labels: *Polymorphic,* (or "Balanced"), *Punctilious, Sublime, Demonstrative, Authoritarian* and *Militant.* The intent of the labels is to emphasize the very different tenors of each of the distributions of character types.

Table A3 demonstrates that:

- Relatively small changes in gene frequencies could cause large changes in the phenotype frequencies.

- The frequencies of non-viable P and null types are low for these habitancies, on the order of 0 to 8 percent.

Evolutionary origins of NPA traits

The assumption of a genetic basis for the traits N, P and A implies that their origins reside in the evolution of humans from precursor species, and in particular, that the traits are likely to be found in primates other than *Homo sapiens.* As examples, the model leads to proposed character types as follows:

- The omnivorous, hierarchal, unsmiling olive baboon, known for its lengthy grooming rituals, would be a likely perfectionist-aggressive PA type (Fig. A4).

- The herbivorous, aloof, phlegmatic orangutan and gorilla, capable of gingival smiles, would be likely NP types.

Relative incidence of phenotypes on basis of gene frequencies n, p and a	
Phenotype	*Relative incidence*
N	$n^2 \times (1-p)^2 \times (1-a^2)$
A	$(1-n^2) \times (1-p)^2 \times a^2$
NP	$n^2 \times p(2-p) \times (1-a^2)$
NA	$n^2 \times (1-p)^2 \times a^2$
PA	$(1-n^2) \times p(2-p) \times a^2$
NPA	$n^2 \times p(2-p) \times a^2$
P	$2n(1-n) \times p(2-p) \times 2a(1-a)$
null (0)	$2n(1-n) \times (1-p)^2 \times 2a(1-a)$

Table A2. Relative incidences of phenotypes for the first generation. The incidence for each phenotype is the product of three probabilities, corresponding to the presence or absence of the three traits N, P and A. The P and null types contribute neither to parentage nor issue.

	HABITANCY					
Phenotype	**Balanced**	**Punctilious**	**Sublime**	**Demonstrative**	**Authoritarian**	**Militant**
N	7	3	77	2	1	1
A	3	<1	<1	2	17	34
NP	22	78	18	7	2	1
NA	13	<1	3	20	6	11
PA	9	2	<1	7	52	35
NPA	39	8	1	61	17	12
P	4	8	<1	1	4	2
null (0)	1	<1	1	<1	1	2
Gene frequencies	$n = 0.90$ $p = 0.50$ $a = 0.80$	$n = 0.90$ $p = 0.80$ $a = 0.30$	$n = 0.99$ $p = 0.10$ $a = 0.20$	$n = 0.95$ $p = 0.50$ $a = 0.95$	$n = 0.50$ $p = 0.50$ $a = 0.95$	$n = 0.50$ $p = 0.30$ $a = 0.95$

Table A3. Frequencies of phenotypes in six habitancies (per 100 zygotes, or pregnancies). The P and null (0) phenotypes are non-viable. Non-viable types arise when the zygote has neither trait N nor A. The above analysis is confined to Dominant character types on the assumption of two alleles for each NPA gene.

Fig. A4. The NPA model proposes that the olive baboon is a likely perfectionist-aggressive PA type.

- Akin to humans, the omnivorous, promiscuous chimpanzee, also capable of the gingival smile, would likely have a heterogeneous distribution of types, with NA and NPA types predominating.

Predictive aspects of NPA model

The model would have the potential to be predictive in the following categories:

- The possible genetic character types of children could be deduced from the character types of parents.

- Relations could be defined between genetic character type and susceptibility to certain physical and mental diseases.

- Combinations of parental character types prone to infertility problems (miscarriage and stillbirth) could be identified, these combinations being ones which permit the occurrence of a fetus having neither trait N nor A.

- Allele frequencies for the NPA traits, as well as the resultant distributions of NPA character types, in various societies could be analyzed on the basis of well-known principles of population genetics.
- Studies with primates could confirm a biological basis for behavior in the areas of sociobiology and evolutionary psychology.

Criticism and controversy

Controversy has always followed past positions taken by the scientific community relating human behavior to inheritance, as in Arthur Jensen's theories of intelligence, Herrnstein and Murray's "The Bell Curve", or Lewontin and colleagues' "Not in Our Genes". The NPA personality model is not exempt. The result of the "nature versus nurture" debate has been that a gauntlet had been thrown to those who espouse genetic underpinnings to behavior: "show us the relevant genes".

The slow progress of unraveling of the genetic basis of personality is the subject of a review article by Jang and colleagues [2]. They point out the lack of any genetic framework in the classification of the Diagnostics and Statistical Manual of American psychiatry (DSM-IV), and the pressing need to identify "genetically crisp" characteristics — or genetic traits of behavior that are independent of competing genetic and environmental influences.

The NPA model posits narcissism — as expressed by sanguinity — to be a genetic trait, being related to the parasympathetic branch of the autonomic nervous system, just as aggression is classically related to the sympathetic branch. This concept of narcissism, and the associated narcissistic rage, is not found in any branch of classical medicine or psychiatry and remains a key point requiring validation. Of note is a study by Livesley and colleagues [3] with identical and fraternal twins. They found that of a total of eighteen dimensions of personality it was narcissism that had the highest heritability.

The manuscript of the NPA model was copyrighted with the Library of Congress in 1982, being published in book form in 1985 [17] and in a peer-reviewed journal in 1990 [6]. A revised electronic edition was released in 2004 and the online NPA personality test in 2005. Studies are in progress utilizing the NPA personality test in obstetric and gynecological patients [18].

Although the NPA model is several decades old, it has not been validated in the sense of withstanding scrutiny by the scientific method — as is true of all other theories of personality as well. Given the recent advances in deciphering the human genome, such scrutiny may soon be possible. The ideas of Karen Horney have been resilient over time, and the validity of her observations that form the basis of the NPA model awaits the relevant studies in the realm of behavioral genetics.

References

Benis, A.M. *Toward Self and Sanity: On the genetic origins of the human character*, Psychological Dimensions, New York, 1985. ISBN 0884370747 [2nd edition, *The NPA Theory of Personality*, 2017. ISBN 9781521283295]

Benis, A.M. and J.H. Rand (1986). A model of human personality based on Mendelian genetics (abstract). *Proceedings of the American Association for the Advancement of Science,* Publication 86-5, 124.

Benis, A.M. (1990). A theory of personality traits leads to a genetic model for borderline types and schizophrenia. *Speculations in Science and Technology 13* (3), 167-175.

Freud, Sigmund. "Heredity and the aetiology of the neuroses," in *Early Psycho-analytic Publications,* Hogarth, London, [1896] 1962.

Horney, Karen. *Neurosis and Human Growth*, Norton, 1950.

Horney, Karen. *Our Inner Conflicts*, Norton, 1945.

Horney, Karen. *New Ways in Psychoanalysis*, Norton, 1939.

Horney, Karen. *Feminine Psychology*, Norton, [1922 to 1937] 1967.

Jang, K.L., Vernon, P.A. and W.J. Livesley (2001). Behavioural-genetic perspectives on personality function. *Canadian Journal of Psychiatry 46*, 234-244.

Livesley, W.J., Jang, K.L., Jackson, D.N. and P.A. Vernon (1993). Genetic and environmental contributions to dimensions of personality disorder. *American Journal of Psychiatry 150*, 1826-1831.

Stone, Michael H. *The Borderline Syndromes*, McGraw-Hill, 1980.

Citations

1. *Personality*, in Wikipedia.

2. Jang *et al.* (2001). Behavioural-genetic perspectives.

3. Livesley *et al.* (1993). Genetic and environmental contributions.

4. Horney, *Neurosis and Human Growth*, Chapter 8: The expansive solutions: the appeal of mastery.

5. Horney, *Neurosis and Human Growth*, Chapter 4: Neurotic pride.

6. Benis (1990). Theory of personality traits leads to genetic model.

7. Horney, *New Ways in Psychoanalysis*, Chapter 5: The concept of narcissism.

8. Horney, *Our Inner Conflicts*, Chapter 4: Moving against people.

9. Horney, *Feminine Psychology*, pp. 182-213.

10. Horney, *New Ways in Psychoanalysis*, p. 97.

11. Horney, *Our Inner Conflicts*, Chapter 12: Sadistic trends.

12. Horney, *New Ways in Psychoanalysis*, Chapter 15: Masochistic phenomena.

13. Horney, *Our Inner Conflicts*, Chapter 3: Moving toward people.

14. Horney, *Our Inner Conflicts*, Chapter 5: Moving away from people.

15. Horney, *Neurosis and Human Growth*, Chapter 10: Morbid dependency.

16. Benis, *Toward Self and Sanity*, Chapter 10: Genetics.

17. Benis, *Toward Self and Sanity.*

18. by Donna K. Hobgood, M.D., Clinical Attending Physician, University of Tennessee College of Medicine, Chattanooga.

Illustrations

Karen Horney: "Studio photo" courtesy of Karen Horney Papers, Manuscripts and Archives, Yale University Library, New Haven.

Character types according to theory of humors: From Johann Kaspar Lavater, *Physiognomics*, ca. 1775.

Olive baboon: U.S. Fish and Wildlife Service.

Source

This article originally appeared in *Wikipedia*, the online encyclopedia in May 2006. It was later deleted for reasons of non-notability. The reference was: "NPA personality theory", *Wikipedia, The Free Encyclopedia,* 2 July 2006, Wikimedia Foundation:

http://en.wikipedia.org/wiki/NPA_personality_theory.

GLOSSARY

aggression   The basis of human desire to survive by maintaining a position of power over competitors. Trait A of the model.

aggressive rage (A rage)   Mass discharge of the sympathetic nervous system related to the A trait of aggression.

allele   An alternative form of a gene at a given locus

association   The occurrence together, in a family or population, of two characteristics in a frequency greater than that predicted by chance. The association may or may not reside in the expression of linked genes.

assortative mating   Non-random or preferential mating among individuals of a population.

autistic   Developmental disorders characterized by restricted and repetitive behavior that impair social interaction and communication.

autonomic nervous system   The portion of the nervous system governing many activities that are not under conscious control. It is composed of two parts: the *sympathetic* and *parasympathetic* nervous systems.

autosomal   Pertaining to a non-sex chromosome.

bipolar disorder   A major disorder of the emotional tone of the individual. It is characterized by severe mood swings toward mania, depression or both.

blushing   A response of flushing in an emotional context, in the skin of the face, neck and upper chest. According to the model, individuals having the N trait have an increased predisposition to blushing and flushing.

Borderline NPA type   An NPA type in which neither trait N nor A is fully expressed.

breed true   A trait is said to breed true if two parents of the same phenotype always produce offspring of that same phenotype exclusively. The NA type is the only type of the model that always breeds true: any two NA types can have only NA offspring.

carrier   An individual who carries a gene that is not expressed. In the model, the non-aggressive N and NP types can be carriers of genes for the A⁻ trait of inhibited aggression.

chromosomes The cell structures containing the genetic material DNA. The human genome is composed of 46 chromosomes: 22 pairs of autosomes and 2 sex chromosomes.

cognition The acts of thinking, feeling, knowing, reasoning and learning, including both awareness and judgment.

complementary genes Genes that produce different phenotypic effects depending on whether they are present separately or together.

compliant type A Passive Aggressive character type having profound inhibition of the A trait (denoted by A=).

dominant trait Refers to Mendelian dominance. Not to be confused with *Dominant type*.

Dominant type An NPA type in which the traits N and/or A are fully expressed. The six types are: N, A, NA, NP, PA and NPA.

ectomorph Tall and lean *somatotype*, as described by psychologist William Sheldon in the 1940's.

energetic state An individual having the A− trait can assume a transient energetic state resembling dominance (A+) by undergoing a *personality split*.

exhibitionism Tendency toward display or extravagant behavior. Exhibitionism is most often a manifestation of the unbridled N trait.

explosive personality A disorder characterized by volcanic outbursts of rage, or of verbal or physical aggressiveness.

expressivity The degree to which a genetic trait is observed in the phenotype. Variable expressivity may be caused by modifier genes or by environmental effects.

extrovert An individual whose attention and interests are directed primarily toward others.

failure to thrive Refers to an infant who does not develop normally and eventually succumbs.

"fight-or-fight" reaction Behavioral response associated with mass discharge of the *sympathetic nervous system*.

gene A fundamental unit of heredity, composed mainly of DNA. Genes are arranged in linear order on the chromosomes.

gene frequency The probability of an allele's existing at a given chromosomal locus in an individual of a given population.

genotype   The genetic constitution of alleles in an individual with respect to a gene locus or loci.

geographic trail   A set of connected geographic points corresponding to the location of the birth of parents in successive generations where a particular dominant trait or marker is passed from parent to child.

gingival smile   A broad smile, revealing the gums of the upper teeth, related to the N trait.

habitancy   In NPA population genetics, the inhabitants of a region, taken collectively, or a subpopulation. For ease of communication, we define the following habitancies:

Polymorphic — a mixture of NPA character types
Sublime — mainly N types
Punctilious — … NP types
Corybantic — … NA types
Demonstrative — … NPA types
Authoritarian — … PA types
Militant — … A types
Introspective — … NPA– types

The Authoritarian and Militant habitancies have high prevalences of non-sanguine types; the others have primarily sanguine types. Some examples are: *Polymorphic:* USA, UK, South Africa, Australia. *Sublime:* East Africa, Mongolia, areas of India, Polynesian Islands. *Punctilious:* Northern Italy, Switzerland, Germany, Korea, areas of Scandinavia and China, Taiwan, indigenous Yucatan and Arctic. *Corybantic:* Brazil, West Africa, indigenous tribes in New Guinea, Melanesia and Aboriginal Australia. *Demonstrative:* Southern Italy and France, Northern Iran, Colombia. *Authoritarian:* Western Russia, Eastern Europe, Balkans. *Militant:* Yemen and Arab region of Iraq. *Introspective:* Finland, Newfoundland, Scotland, New Zealand, Tasmania.

Hardy-Weinberg approach   A mathematical scheme by which it is possible to compute the relative prevalence of phenotypes on the basis of assumed gene frequencies in a population at equilibrium.

Horney, Karen (1885–1952)   German-American psychiatrist of Dutch and Norwegian heritage.

hybrid   An individual whose parents belong to two different varieties of a species, or to two different species.

hypomanic In psychiatric terms, an individual who has a heightened emotional tone. In *mania* the individual is psychotic and usually requires hospitalization.

infertility   The relative inability of a mated couple to produce viable offspring.

introvert An individual whose interests are predominantly concerned with his own mental life.

lethal gene   A gene that renders non-viable an organism or cell possessing it. According to the present model, the genes corresponding to the absence of traits N and A, when present together, act as *complementary genes* to produce a lethal effect (a nonviable zygote).

modifier genes   Genes that modify an observed physical or behavioral trait.

morbid dependency   A symbiotic relationship based on the trait of aggression, essentially sadomasochistic in nature, between individuals assuming dominant and submissive roles.

mutation   A change in the DNA structure of a gene. If the change occurs in a gamete, then the alteration may be perpetuated in subsequent generations.

narcissism   From Narcissus, the figure in Greek mythology who fell in love with his own reflected image. In the present model, narcissism is related to the N trait of sanguinity.

narcissistic arms gesture   A gesture of recognition in which the arms are extended to the front or sides, with the fingers slightly spread apart.

narcissistic personality disorder (NPD)   In the NPA model patients diagnosed with NPD will likely be individuals having the *unbridled* N trait.

narcissistic rage (N rage)   Mass discharge of the autonomic nervous system related to the N trait of sanguinity.

non-compliant type   A Passive Aggressive character type having partial inhibition of the A trait (denoted by A−).

non-sanguine   Refers to individuals who lack the trait N.

null zygote   According to the model, a zygote in which none of the NPA traits are expressed. Null zygotes do not develop into viable individuals.

paranoia A behavioral pattern characterized by hyper-sensitivity, suspicion, jealousy, envy and a tendency to blame others and ascribe evil motives to them.

"passive-aggressive" A behavioral pattern characterized by obstructionism, procrastination and intentional inefficiency. Not to be confused with *Passive Aggressive type.*

Passive Aggressive type An NPA type in which trait A is genetically partially inhibited.

perfectionism The P trait of the model, appearing in behavior as 1) the achievement of order by persistence and repetition, and 2) as a trait that modulates the expression of the unbridled N and A traits.

personality A collection of behavioral patterns unique to an individual that is consistent over time.

personality split According to the model, individuals having the A or A− trait may transiently assume the converse subdued (A−) and energetic (A+) states, respectively.

phenotype The observable traits in an individual. The NPA character types (N, A, NP, NA−, etc.) are phenotypes.

"playing the game" Individuals having a measure of the trait of aggression constantly "play the game" of dominance and submission.

pleiotropism The determination of multiple characteristics by a single gene.

power behind throne A symbiotic relationship between a PA individual (the Power) and a figurehead individual on whom he depends.

psychosis A major mental disorder in which the individual's ability to interpret reality is grossly impaired.

recessive trait Refers to a trait that is expressed only when the causative gene is present on both chromosomes of an autosomal pair.

resignation The state denoted −A in which an individual at maturity renounces the "playing of the game" of dominance and submission and adopts a philosophy of serene independence.

Resigned type An NPA type in which trait A (aggression) is inhibited by environmental factors after maturity in an individual who was formerly either 1) a Dominant A, PA, NA or NPA type, or 2) a Passive Aggressive type.

sadism Satisfaction derived from aggressively dominating or abusing others.

sadomasochism A symbiotic relationship between two individuals based on the trait of aggression.

sanguine, sanguinity According to ancient physiology, belonging to one of the "four temperaments" in which blood predominates over the other three "humors", leading to a ruddy countenance and exuberant behavior. In the NPA model a sanguine personality type is any type having the N trait.

schizoid Withdrawn; tending to avoid close relationships with others.

schizophrenia A group of psychotic disorders characterized by disturbances in thought, mood and behavior. In the present model, a kind of schizophrenia may occur in an individual if there is a lack of normal expression of both the N and A traits.

smile According to the model, the social smile of recognition is based on the N trait of sanguinity.

somatotype Classification of physique (body types) developed by psychologist William Sheldon in the 1940's.

subdued state An individual having fully expressed trait A can be reduced to a transient subdued state resembling submission (A–) by undergoing a *personality split.*

subjugated state A chronic state resembling submission (A–) of an individual with respect to a stronger companion or mate.

Submissive type A compliant Passive Aggressive character type who adopts a life style of deference to others.

symbiosis A relationship between two individuals that has elements of mutual advantage.

sympathetic nervous system A division of the autonomic nervous system that controls the "fight-or-flight" response related to the trait of aggression.

synergy An enhanced effect on behavior, for example when the unbridled N and A traits complement each other in the NA type.

temperament The general level of activity, reactivity or excitability of an individual in the Pavlovian sense.

unbridled trait The presence of fully expressed trait N or A without modulation by the P trait.

SOURCES OF ILLUSTRATIONS

PART 1 — Theory

1   From Benis (1985, 2017d). See also the Appendix.

2   Drawings by Anthony Moore, from Desmond Morris (1977): *Manwatching*. Courtesy of Elsevier/Equinox, Oxford.

3   The four characters of man, from Johann Kaspar Lavater's *Physiognomics* (*ca.* 1775).

4   "Microcosm diagram of the mind," from Robert Fludd (*ca.* 1617): *Utriusque cosmi maioris scilicet et minoris metaphysica...*

5   By Andrea Laurel. Creative Commons (CC) license via: flickr.com/photos/81461206@N02/7489708130.

6   By kambodza. Creative Commons license via: flickr.com/photos/49507393@N08/4535874193.

7   From Benis (1985, 2017d).

8   From Benis A.M. (2018). *The Enigma of Short Parents Who Have Tall Children*. KDP/Amazon.

9   Bridal couple with their parents, by Katherine Hala. Creative Commons license via: flickr.com/photos/kahala/4501198519.

10   *Abraham Lincoln*, by Bill Oberst Jr. Creative Commons license via: flickr.com/photos/billoberstjr/6940092689. *Vladimir Putin*, from magspace.ru: uploads/2014/09/08/00-10PutinLookingAt18.jpg.

11   From Benis (1985, 2017d).

PART 2 — Sanguinity: The N trait

12   By max_thinks_sees. Creative Commons license via: flickr.com/photos/hundreds/2830576097.

13   "The last curtain call," by canhasal. Creative Commons license via: flickr.com/photos/canhasal/9518165735.

14   Amsterdam station, by Matthew Kenwrick. Creative Commons license via: flickr.com/photos/58847482@N03/5597908738.

15   By Mihai Paraschiv, Bucharest/Romania. From Pexels: pexels.com/photos/99568/smile-portrait-beauty-girl-99568.jpeg.

16   From Benis (1985/2017).

17   By Lucas Mohamd. Creative Commons license via: flickr.com/photos/147946400@N02/33291582525.

18   By House of Praise. Creative Commons license via: flickr.com/photos/rccghouseofpraise/8448212019.

19   Still from *Encore* (1951). Courtesy of the Rank Organisation, London.

20   By Hans G. Bäckman. Creative Commons license via: flickr.com/photos/koxa74/17058437839.

21   By Anne-Lise Heinrichs. Creative Commons license via: flickr.com/photos/snigl3t/3166256303.

22   By M. Doss. Creative Commons license via: flickr.com/photos/snigl3t/3166256303.

23   From Pexels, "English" via: pixabay.com/en/tattoos-adult-body-art-couple-girl-1867535.

24   By T.C. Manasan. Creative Commons license via: flickr.com/photos/trishamanasan/4799364388.

25   "Purple gallinule chick, Florida" by Henry T. McLin. Creative Commons license via: flickr.com/photos/hmclin/7121257091.

26   By Disney/ABC Television Group/Adam Taylor. CC license via: flickr.com/photos/disneyabc/14212167336.

PART 3 — Perfectionism: the P trait

27   By Lee Herrera. Creative Commons license via: flickr.com/photos/20343090@N00/7350405030.

28   North Korean festival. By Laika. From Wikipedia: en.wikipedia.org/wiki/Arirang_Festival#/media/File:Laika_ac_Arirang_Mass_Games_(7934639696).jpg.

29   By Richard Fisher. Creative Commons license via: flickr.com/photos/richardfisher/4269668407.

30   "Eric Vollrath Beetle Collection." By Justin Sewell. CC license via: flickr.com/photos/ianmalcm/27027150862.

31   *Top:* Tuscany manuscript. By Grant Barclay, Glasgow. Creative Commons license via: flickr.com/photos/grantbarclay/40102512110. *Bottom:* Stan Kenton and Buddy Childers, Richmond, Va., 1947 or 1948. By Wm. P. Gottlieb via: flickr.com/photos/library_of_congress/4843134923.

32   Ginza district, by Matthew Kenwrick. Creative Commons license via: flickr.com/photos/58847482@N03/5774814801.

33   2013 K-pop World Festival in Changwon. By Republic of Korea via: flickr.com/photos/koreanet/11039813825.

34   By Igor Link, Offenbach am Main/Germany. From Pexels via: pixabay.com/en/hiringc-feedback-analytics-profile-2697952.

35   By Min An, Ho Chi Minh City/Vietnam. From: pexels.com/photo/woman-wearing-white-red-and-green-cold-shoulder-dress-1163196.

PART 4 — Aggression: The A trait

36   Billboard of Ayatollah Khomeini and Ali Khamenei. By humbleslave. Creative Commons license via: flickr.com/photos/humbelslave/4459337291.

37   Drawings by Patricia Moss-Vreeland. From Benis (1985/2017).

38   By Fredrik Lindström. Creative Commons license via: flickr.com/photos/frli/3533457738.

39   By Nika Vee. Creative Commons license via: flickr.com/photos/nika/69796982.

40   *Top:* Peter the Great interrogating his son. Nineteenth century painting by Nikolai Ge, Tretyakov Gallery, Moscow. *Bottom:* From Bundesarchiv, Bild 183-S38324 via Wikipedia.

41   By David Goehring. Creative Commons license via: flickr.com/photos/isthmene/3215365427.

42   By Intel Free Press. Creative Commons license via: flickr.com/photos/intelfreepress/8294794328.

43   Photo by Mikhail Metzel/AFP. From inmediahk. CC license via: flickr.com/photos/inmediahk/7179309299.

44   By Apionid. Creative Commons license via: flickr.com/photos/apionid/24010731305.

45   Photo by Alexander Vysotsky, Baikonur. By NASA Johnson. CC license via: flickr.com/photos/nasa2explore/30434126460.

46   By Rolands Lakis *(top)*. Creative Commons license via: flickr.com/photos/rolandslakis/147479380, and Konstantin Lazorkin *(bottom)*. Creative Commons license via: flickr.com/photos/slayer23/6192299758.

47   By Julie F. Creative Commons license via: flickr.com/photos/fisticuffs/4600097.

48   "General Schwarzkopf speaks with troops supporting Operation Desert Shield"via Wikipedia: /wiki/Norman_Schwarzkopf_Jr.

PART 5 — Inhibition of Aggression: The A⁻ Trait

49   By Poonam Agarwal. Creative Commons license via: flickr.com/photos/poonamagarwal/8487448549.

50   By Isthmene Yoshizawa. Creative Commons license via: flickr.com/photos/isthmene/3215365427.

51   Still from *Quartet* (1948). Courtesy of the Rank Organisation, London.

52   By Julie Laurent. Creative Commons license via: flickr.com/photos/julielaurent/5994748056.

53   By Neil Moralee. Creative Commons license via: flickr.com/photos/neilmoralee/8610246577.

PART 6 — Inversions: Pseudo-aggression and Pseudo-narcissism

54   "Ritton". By Flexgraph, France. Creative Commons license via: flickr.com/photos/flexgraph/3128499795.

55   By Konstantin Lazorkin. Creative Commons license via: flickr.com/photos/slayer23/4756171226.

56   Photo by Dean Stockings (2013) from Wikipedia commons. *Inset:* Album cover, *Culture Club – Kissing To Be Clever* (1982) from chris m. Creative Commons license via: flickr.com/photos/photos/rzrxtion/5186779033.

PART 7 — Caricatures of the Character Types

57   Barack Obama by DonkeyHotey via Wikipedia Commons File: 2012 Obama Romney caricature.jpg.

58   By Rachel Swallows (Swallows Gallery): "Elven Princess". CC license via: flickr.com/photos/falconghost/26903293683.

59   By SilviaP_Design via: pixabay.com/en/woman-angry-emotion-face-evil-1808669.

60   "Conceited" from IsraGarcia18. Creative Commons license via: flickr.com/photos/138349603@N03/32672211143.

61   By June Yarham, UK. Lady in red dress by Jon Paul Photoarts. CC license via: flickr.com/photos/junibears/42385944502.

62   By Lauren Gledhill, Fidget Photography, Wrexham/Wales/UK. Creative Commons license via: flickr.com/photos/fidget_photography/5425136010.

63   From George UK via: pixabay.com/en/females-pin-up-girl-fashion-people-1450050.

64   Vladimir Putin by DonkeyHotey via: Wikipedia Commons
      File: Vladimir Putin –Olympic Host.jpg.

65   By RyanMcGuire. From Pexels via:
      pixabay.com/en/man-fashion-model-fashion-man-930397.

66   Angela Merkel by DonkeyHotey. Creative Commons license
      via: flickr.com/photos/donkeyhotey/12952652895.

67   By Szilárd Szabó, Pápa/Hungary. From Pexels via:
      pixabay.com/en/people-men-thinker-group-3407083.

68   Richard Cheney by DonkeyHotey. Creative Commons license
      via: flickr.com/photos/donkeyhotey/16011605976.

69   From Pixabay, via Pexels:
      pexels.com/photo/fashion-person-woman-model-47859.

70   From Charlebois. Public domain via:
      flickr.com/photos/48386740@N08/30578118947.

71   Robert Mitchum. Public domain via:
      wikimedia.org/wiki/File:Robert_Mitchum_1949.jpg.

72   Christopher Christie by DonkeyHotey. Creative Commons
      license via: flickr.com/photos/donkeyhotey/9529109477.

73   Illustration by John Tenniel from "Alice's Adventures in
      Wonderland" by Lewis Carroll, 1865.

74   By Simon Ishmael Cliff. Creative Commons license via:
      flickr.com/photos/sicliff/10747079405.

75   John Bolton by DonkeyHotey. Creative Commons license via:
      flickr.com/photos/donkeyhotey/27312467408.

76   Native American Chief Phizi Gall, by David Frances Barry
      (1854-1934). Public domain via:
      museumsyndicate.com/item.76892.

77   By Mayeli Espinosa Rios at Cali/Colombia. Creative Commons
      license via: flickr.com/photos/106661345@N07/11597656163.

78   Jerry Lewis, from "The Nutty Professor." Graphite drawing of
      publicity photograph by Dean Huck. Creative Commons
      license via: flickr.com/photos/40306046@N05/18317693226.

79   Bill Maher by DonkeyHotey. Creative Commons license via:
      flickr.com/photos/donkeyhotey/5553736775.

80   "My tribute to Leonard Nimoy (1931 - 2015)" by Roberto
      Rizzato. Creative Commons license via:
      flickr.com/photos/rizzato/3036985567.

81   From Pamela Russell via: pixabay.com/photos/josephine-baker-portrait-vintage-3668075.

82   By Oliana Gruzdeva, Novokuznetsk/Siberia/Russia. Via pixabay.com/en/woman-fashion-lovely-girl-young-3406357.

83   By Sue Cro. Creative Commons license via: flickr.com/photos/31018850@N04/36453116200.

84   From Amy Z, USA via pixabay.com/en/couple-love-rose-laughing-happy-3375701.

84   From BBW Hunter, "Sweet Felina." Creative Commons license via: flickr.com/photos/153741272@N07/39215072261.

85   From Pexels, "English" via: pixabay.com/en/adult-affection-facial-expression-2178963.

87   Elizabeth Warren by DonkeyHotey. Creative Commons license via: flickr.com/photos/donkeyhotey/13906218886.

88   Narendra Modi by DonkeyHotey. Creative Commons license via: flickr.com/photos/donkeyhotey/14036449217.

89   Michael Jackson. Wikipedia images via: fr.wikipedia.org/wiki/Filmographie_de_Michael_Jackson.

90   Charles Darwin *ca.* 1854, via Wikipedia Commons file: Charles Darwin seated crop.jpg.

91   From Petra Bauman, Slovenia. High contrast image from color original via: pexels.com/photo/woman-in-white-top-and-gold-colored-necklace-1377183.

92   By Nebojsa Mladjenovic, St. Leger/Vauban/France. CC license via: flickr.com/photos/mladjenovic_n/4601084173.

93   "Solitary Involvement" by Greg Nissen. Creative Commons license via: flickr.com/photos/gregoryniss/4488495028.

PART 8 — Historical Figures

94   Portrait of Napoleon in his study, by Jacques-Louis David. Courtesy of National Gallery of Art, Washington D.C.

95   Photograph by Alexander Hesler, June 3, 1860. Courtesy of the Chicago Historical Society.

96   Daguerreotype by N.H. Shepherd, the Library of Congress.

97   Portrait by Hans Holbein, the younger. Courtesy of the Thyssen-Bornemisza Collection.

98   Portrait by M. Sittow. Kunsthistorisches Museum, Vienna. Via en.wikipedia.org/wiki/Catherine_of_Aragon.

99	*Charles I*: portrait by Van Dyck at Windsor Castle. By courtesy of H.M. the Queen. *Richelieu*: portrait by Champaigne. By permission of the Trustees, The National Gallery, London.

100	Portrait by Pesne. Courtesy of Verwaltung der Staatlichen Schlosser und Garten, Schloss Charlottenburg, Berlin.

101	Imperial War Museum via: en.wikipedia.org/ wiki/ Grigori_Rasputin#/media/File:Grigori_Rasputin_1916.jpg.

102	Archival photograph of Joseph Stalin. Accessed via: www.pinterest.com.

103	Adolf Hitler, with Mussolini's son-in-law, Count Galeazzo Ciano. From photo colorized by Jared Enos. CC license via: flickr.com/photos/jenoscolor/16227955056.

104	From Waiting For The Word. Creative Commons license via: flickr.com/photos/waitingfortheword/5572555297.

PART 9 — Couples

105	"American Gothic" by Grant Wood, 1929 via Wikipedia: en.wikipedia.org/wiki/American_Gothic#/media/File.

106	By Oliana Gruzdeva, Novokuznetsk/Siberia/Russia. Via pixabay.com/en/couple-love-kiss-sweethearts-3433754.

107	*Top:* by Krista Guenin, Woburn/MA. CC license via: flickr.com/photos/ kristaphoto/6872309925.
	Bottom: Wedding, Sofia/Bulgaria by Rosendr. CC license via: flickr.com/photos/91883729@N03/9182661864.

108	By Ashley Webb, Los Angeles. Creative Commons license via flickr.com/photos/xlordashx/10085930253.

109	Roman Polanski and Sharon Tate (Cannes, 1968). Photo by Jack Garofalo. From Lily Laurent. Public domain via: flickr.com/photos/147314555@N04/33740951494.

110	By Frankie Cordoba, Miami/Florida via: unsplash.com/ photos/FEdRvNu2fd0.

111	*Top:* Stan Laurel and Oliver Hardy with Lupe Vélez in "Hollywood Party" (1934). *Bottom:* Ralph Kramden (Jackie Gleason) and Alice Kramden (Audrey Meadows) in a "Honeymooners" scene. Both via Wikipedia Commons.

112	By Nathan Dumlao via: unsplash.com/photos/q6cs6C3SaaQ.

113	From Capitol Records: soundtrack album of "The King and I". Via wikipedia/en/8/86/The_King_and_I.

114   The Shook Twins from San Francisco in 2015, by Jay Blakesberg via: wikipedia/commons/0/01/Shook_twins.

115   By Min An, Ho Chi Minh City/Vietnam via: pexels.com/photo/man-looking-at-mirror-1134184.

PART 10 — Children of the World

116   From Omar Medina Films, Santo Domingo/Dominican Republic via: pixabay.com/en/family-women-man-posing-child-1434722.

117   From jimmyjatt1993 via: pixabay.com/en/child-girl-portrait-christmas-1942559.

118   From Ruslan Gilmanshin, Moscow/Russia via: pixabay.com/en/girl-young-blue-eyes-eyes-look-510446.

119   "The Virgin of the Grapes," by Pierre Mignard (1612-95). Louvre Museum. Via Wikipedia Commons.

120   Fresco at St. Isaac's Cathedral (completed in 1858), Petrograd/Russia.

121   From Dariusz Sankowski, Wrocław/Poland via: pixabay.com/en/boy-child-portrait-military-weapon-958477.

122   From Chelsea Ferenando, Tampa/FL/USA via: unsplash.com/photos/Qh0yZF1vKQA.

123   From Pam Simon, Orange/TX/USA via pixabay.com/en/ballerina-beauty-costume-tutu-1618765.

124   From Alexis León, Santiago/Chile via: pixabay.com/en/users/AlexisLeon-1398503.

125   By Rod Waddington. Creative Commons license via: flickr.com/photos/rod_waddington/8539773209.

126   "The well." By Christopher Michel. Creative Commons license via: flickr.com/photos/cmichel67/32404887423.

127   "Faces of Zambia" from Alex Berger, USA/Denmark. CC license via: flickr.com/photos/virtualwayfarer/ 7931415840.

128   "Pyongyang funfair boys" from Roman Harak, Slovakia. CC license via: flickr.com/photos/roman-harak/5944137982.

129   *Top:* From Analise Benevides, Las Vegas/USA via: unsplash.com/photos/E4ugS9F8Was. *Bottom:* From Dorothy Loges, Tunas/MO/USA via: pixabay.com/en/baby-glasses-cute-happy-child- kid-204185.

130   From Barry Lenard, Broken Arrow/OK/USA. CC license via: flickr.com/photos/babybare11/10980961716.

PART 11 — Origins & Geography

131   By Brad. Creative Commons license via: flickr.com/photos/bfra07/8344982453.

132   By Paolo Macorig. Creative Commons license via: flickr.com/photos/macorig/122557528.

133   By Ryan Summers. Creative Commons license via: flickr.com/photos/oddernod/23709195076.

134   Illustration ©1980 by Margaret LaFarge after photographs of J. Goodall. From John Tyler Bonner: *The Evolution of Culture in Animals.* By permission of the Princeton University Press.

135   By Dan Shouse. Creative Commons license via: flickr.com/photos/danshouse/166273607.

136   Self-portrait taken with the camera of British photographer David Slater. Via wikipedia.org/wiki/Monkey_selfie.

137   By Valerie. Creative Commons license via: flickr.com/photos/ucumari/3344251454.

138   By Fred Dawson. Creative Commons license via: flickr.com/photos/ fwp-dawson/4118971039.

139   By Rusty Stewart. Creative Commons license via: flickr.com/photos/rustystewart/2807165961.

140   By Adam Jason Moore. Creative Commons license via: flickr.com/photos/adamjasonmoore/8704619654.

141   Asokoro section of Abuja, Nigeria. By Mark Fischer. CC license via: flickr.com/photos/fischerfotos/23379499.

142   "Eagle Girl: 13-year-old Ashol-Pan, Mongolia's only female eagle hunter" by David Baxendale. Creative Commons license via: flickr.com/photos/david_baxendale/14523321819.

143   By Rolands Lakis (*top*). Creative Commons license via: flickr.com/photos// rolandslakis/392060768 and by Paval Hadzinski (*bottom*). Creative Commons license via: flickr.com/photos/hadzinski/16609873766.

144   "Across Arabia early 19th century" [*sic*]. By Tribes of the World. Creative Commons license via: flickr.com/photos/92278137@N04/9258576842.

145   By peteropaliu. Creative Commons license via: flickr.com/photos/peteropaliu/8720518470.

146   By Alexander Schimmeck. Creative Commons license via: flickr.com/photos/alschim/14646824606.

147   From the South Dakota Department of Tourism. By Roderick Eime. Creative Commons license via: flickr.com/photos/photos/rodeime/16422452858.

148   "Tupua Polynesian Dance," California/USA. By Joe Utsler. CC license via: flickr.com/photos/crazyunclejoe/4835388835.

149   By Gezelle Rivera (*top*). CC license via: flickr.com/photos/ gezelle/519776952, and by photobom (*bottom*). CC license via: flickr.com/photos/photobom/30781498615.

150   Thai dancer by Sasin Tipchai, Amphoe Phochai/Thailand. From Pexels via: pixabay.com/en/dancer-asia-art-bangkok-pretty-1807516.

151   From PNG Tourism, David Kirkwood. By Roderick Eime. CC license via: flickr.com/photos/rodeime/14294261394.

152   Image by Efes Kitap, Germany. From Pexels via: pixabay.com/en/woman-portrait-face-human-pretty-1747261. Original photograph by Jasmaine Cook, Brooklyn/New York: pixabay.com/en/smile-color-laugh-black-1485850.

153   From photo colorized by Jared Enos. Creative Commons license via: flickr.com/photos/jenoscolor/9422474341.

154   From Benis (1985/2017d).

155   From Benis (1985/2017a,d).

156   From Benis (2017a,d).

157   From Benis (2017a,d).

158   From Benis (2017a,d).

159   *Top: The Genographic Project: Map of Human Migration*, from: genographic.nationalgeographic.com /human-journey. *Bottom:* From Benis (2017a,d).

160   Aztec warriors, as depicted in the Codex Mendoza, *ca.* 1535. Bodelian Library, Oxford. Via Wikipedia/Aztec_warfare.

161   *Top:* By jbdodane. Creative Commons license via: flickr.com/photos/jbdodane/8928374600. See also: slaverysite.com/Body/maps.htm. *Bottom:* See Benis (2017a).

PART 12 — Diversity & Disability

162   From Anastasiya Gepp, Chelyabinsk/Russia via: pixabay.com/en/two-girls-russian-model-beauty-1828539/.

163   By Nathan Penlington, London. Creative Commons license via: flickr.com/photos/nathanpenlington/8057367934.

164   From Wikipedia: en.wikipedia.org/wiki/Daniel_Tammet#/media/File:Bluemet_Tammet.jpg.

165   By Clem Onojeghuo, London/U.K. From Pexels: pexels.com/photo/man-wearing-silver-skull-ring-194087.

166   Photo taken August 14, 2017. California Department of Corrections and Rehabilitation via: Wikipedia/MansonB33920.

167   By Alessandro Baffa, Golfe-Juan/France. Creative Commons license via: flickr.com/photos/alebaffa/9712816404.

168   By Gerd Altmann, Freiburg/Germany via: pixabay.com/en/woman-face-psychosis-head-hands-565132.

169   "An eight-year-old boy with Down syndrome." From Wikipedia: en.wikipedia.org/wiki/Down_syndrome.

170   By Flavio Spugna. Creative Commons license via: flickr.com/photos/fspugna/20347223721.

171   From Craig Duffy. Creative Commons license via: flickr.com/photos/pinkcowphotography/8096213477.

172   By Reid Rosenberg. Creative Commons license via: flickr.com/photos/reid_rosenberg/5616618789.

173   "Chaos." By Richard Yu, Creative Commons license via: flickr.com/photos/wojohowitz/3323482787.

174   U.S. Army Signal Corps photo (Mullin). Creative Commons license via: flickr.com/photos/imcomkorea/3192739923.

175   Male Parkinson's victim, 1892. From *Nouvelle Iconographie de la Salpêtrière*, Vol V. National Library of Medicine, Bethesda/MD. Via /catalog/nlm:nlmuid-101435392-img.

176   By Sarahluv/London/UK. Creative Commons license via: flickr.com/photos/sarahluv/3803998500.

177   By Julián D Gaitán, Armenia/Colombia. Creative Commons license via: flickr.com/photos/juliangaitan/6213098462.

178   By David Blackwell, "Borderline." Creative Commons license via: flickr.com/photos/mobilestreetlife/5765352153.

179   By Dmitry Sladkov, Astrakhan/Russia. Creative Commons license via: flickr.com/photos/bg_dn/17433524671.

BIBLIOGRAPHY

Alvarez, L. (2005). Narcissism guides mate selection: Humans mate assortatively, as revealed by facial resemblance, following an algorithm of "self seeking like." *Evolutionary Psychol 2*, 177-94.

Benis, A.M. (1985). *Toward Self & Sanity: On the genetic origins of the human character,* Psychological Dimensions, New York. Revised (2017) as *NPA Theory of Personality*, KDP/Amazon.

Benis A.M. (2017a). *Geographic Distribution of Genetic Character Traits Based on the NPA Theory of Personality*, KDP/Amazon.

Benis A.M. (2017b). *Caricatures of the NPA Personality Types*, KDP/Amazon.

Benis A.M. (2017c). *How Your Personality Type Is Inherited: The NPA Model of Genetic Traits*, KDP/Amazon.

Benis A.M. (2017d). *NPA Personality Theory: The Essentials,* KDP/Amazon.

Benis A.M. (2018). *The Enigma of Short Parents Who Have Tall Children.* KDP/Amazon.

Benis A.M. (1990). A theory of personality traits leads to a genetic model for borderline types and schizophrenia. *Speculations in Science and Technology* 13 (3), 167-75.

Dobzhansky, T. (1970). *Genetics of the Evolutionary Process.* Columbia University Press, New York.

The Genographic Project: Map of Human Migration, National Geographic Society, https://genographic.nationalgeographic.com /human-journey.

Horney K. (1950). *Neurosis and Human Growth*, Norton, New York.

Wahlsten, D. (2012). The hunt for gene effects pertinent to behavioral traits and psychiatric disorders: From mouse to human, *Dev Psychobiol* 54, 475-92.

ABOUT THE AUTHOR

The author received the degree of Doctor of Science from MIT. His medical training was at the Mount Sinai Medical Center in New York, where he served afterward for many years as Research Associate Professor and Director of Cardiothoracic Intensive Care. He is the author of a number of research papers and review articles. His interest in the genetics of personality grew with his experience with families in the intensive care environment.